YEA OR NAY? REFERENDA IN THE UNITED KINGDOM

Quite simply, the fact has to be faced that if we really believe that democracy means some sort of government by the people, our institutions do not make adequate provisions for this today.

Lord Crowther-Hunt and Professor A. T. Peacock, Report of the *Royal Commission on the Constitution Volume II Memorandum of Dissent*

... Hitler's use of the referendum to further totalitarian ends provides no more proof that referenda help would-be dictators than Stalin's use of the Supreme Soviet to support his cult of personality discredits Parliamentary democracy.

Philip Goodhart, *Referendum*

Mr. Speaker: Order. We cannot take a referendum now.

Hansard, December 10, 1969

YEA OR NAY?

Referenda in the United Kingdom

STANLEY ALDERSON

CASSELL : LONDON

Cassell & Co. Ltd—an imprint of
CASSELL & COLLIER MACMILLAN PUBLISHERS LTD
35 Red Lion Square, London WC1R 4SG
Sydney, Auckland, Toronto, Johannesburg

An affiliate of Macmillan Inc., New York

Copyright © Stanley Alderson 1975

First published 1975

Printed in Great Britain by
Northumberland Press Limited, Gateshead

ISBN 0 304 29630 9

CONTENTS

PREFACE

PARTS OF THIS book have appeared in 'The Referendum under the British Constitution' (*Contemporary Review*, November 1973) and 'The Case for Referenda' (*Socialist Commentary*, February 1975). I thank both editors for permission to reprint.

In so far as the information in the book is comprehensive and up-to-date, it is attributable to generous help from embassies, High Commissions, Government Departments, local-authority associations, Town Clerks, librarians, editors, the Labour Party Information Unit and the Conservative Party Research Department.

I am particularly grateful for advice from D. G. C. Allan on the interregnum; John D. Cushing, librarian of the Massachusetts Historical Society, on the Massachusetts Constitutions of 1778 and 1780; David Foulkes and Donald Howell on the referendum conducted by Penarth and District Chamber of Trade; Hans Katzenstein on Swiss law and history; Keith Middlemas on Baldwin's proposed referendum; and Roger Morris on the history of public libraries.

I should be interested to hear of any local referendum (not mentioned in the book) dealing with a subject other than public libraries, Private Bills, pubs and Sunday cinemas. I should be glad to receive ballot-papers from any local referenda whatsoever.

S.A.

1
THE REFERENDUM
IN PERSPECTIVE

'DON'T VOTE IT ONLY ENCOURAGES THEM'.
This is the advice *Peace News* gives its readers at election time. The small staff of *Peace News* work long hours for token salaries. They are informed and compassionate, committed to the reform of society by non-violent means. Their alienation from the parliamentary system should concern us. More constructively, it should remind us of Dicey's conviction that 'the Referendum would bring men to the ballot-box who now hardly vote at all'.[1] James Callaghan was looking at the same problem from the standpoint of Government when he told the 1974 Labour Conference: 'The power structure in Britain is changing. Authority is no longer obeyed for its own sake. There are severe limits on what Government can do.'[2] This is a counsel of despair. If authority is not obeyed for its own sake, some other reason must be found for obeying it. If Government is disobeyed because it is too authoritarian, it must be made more democratic, more participatory.

In the minority report of the Royal (Kilbrandon) Commission on the Constitution, Lord Crowther-Hunt and Professor A. T. Peacock wrote of 'the erosion ... of the extent to which we as a people govern ourselves'.[3] They gave evidence that the British feel they have too little influence, not only on Government, but on local authorities, nationalized industries, the television programmes they watch, the education of their children, and the policies of their employers. Moreover, they feel their influence is generally diminishing. The 'pervading sense of powerlessness'[4] leads to neglect even of the available forms of political participation:

The turnout in our 1970 general election was the lowest since 1945. It was lower than that of nearly every other comparable democracy. And, perhaps most significant of all, the generally declining turnout in Britain between 1950 and 1970 is in contrast to trends in the opposite direction in comparable Western democracies ...

The danger is that this will push us along the road to direct action—possibly violent action—when people and groups believe they have no other alternative to secure what they feel are their just demands ...[5]

1

Most of the comparable Western democracies with higher turnouts in elections do make use of the referendum. Having made the point that 'we, as a people, are more fitted than ever before to govern ourselves',[6] Crowther-Hunt and Peacock concerned themselves primarily with regional devolution. They did, however, draw attention to an interesting opinion poll on the referendum:

> Do you think that the Government of the day should decide all important issues or would you like Britain to adopt a referendum system whereby certain issues are put to the people to decide by popular vote?[7]

The answers to this question in June 1968 were:

	%
Government decide	21
Referendum	69
Don't know	10

A year later people were again asked: 'How should important issues be decided?' The answers were almost identical:

	%
By Government	20
By referendum	68
Don't know	12

In February 1971 a Harris poll asked: 'Do you think we should have a national referendum to decide whether to join the Common Market, or should the Government make the decision?'[8] The replies were 70 per cent for a referendum and 20 per cent for leaving it to the Government. Other polls in 1971 secured substantial majorities in favour of a referendum on the EEC. This was not only before the Labour Party publicized the idea by adopting it as its own policy. It was when 'referendum' was still an unfamiliar term in this country. Opinion Research Centre, in March 1971, asked: 'Do you think it would be a good idea if the Government asked the people to vote *Yes* or *No* before it decided on whether we should go into the Common Market?' The replies were 82 to 14 per cent in favour.[9]

This leaves little doubt of the result if we held a referendum on the referendum.

To understand the alienation of the young, it is not enough to make the traditional distinction between democracy and non-democracy. We must distinguish also between the delegation of authority 'upwards' and 'downwards'. We can envisage an ideal society of free men in which all adults attend a village council, which elects delegates to a county council, which in turn elects delegates to a national council or Parliament. So long as those elected speak and vote only as they are specifically empowered to, they remain true delegates, and all delegation is upwards. As soon as they receive or assume discretion to make their own decisions, they become representatives, issue orders, and delegate authority downwards. At the other extreme, if absolute authority is invested in a hereditary monarch, all delegation is downwards. Historically the two countries that have come closest to these extremes are Switzerland and England.

Delegation upwards is of course the earlier system and was predominant in the moots of Saxon England. After the Norman Conquest, with the unification of England under a single Crown, the Saxon institutions of government were mostly abolished or changed. Folkmoots disappeared. Shiremoots were replaced by courts controlled by lords of the manor, whose judgements were executed by bailiffs (the more important, known as major-bailiffs, giving rise to the title 'mayor'). The counties (or shires) came under the jurisdiction of the sheriffs, who exercised extensive powers as representatives of the King. Ecclesiastical parish meetings survived and were never prevented from discussing civil matters. But the essence of the feudal system was that power derived from the King and was delegated downwards.

What did survive from Saxon to Norman times was the tradition that the King should govern with the advice of his great lords or landholders. William the Conqueror's Great Council included men from the Council of Edward the Confessor. Feudalism was a hierarchical system in which lesser lords (or landholders) swore allegiance to greater, and the greatest to the King himself. To consolidate his power, William the Conqueror required even lesser lords to swear allegiance to himself. He thereby converted England into a single feudal community, in which all the lords owed the duty of attendance and advice in the royal court. Courts, when the King wore his crown, were held at Christmas, Easter and Whitsun. Writs of summons were sent to the lords and there were penalties for non-attendance. A Great Council might be held after a court. The thrice-yearly courts were possible only because England was a small country.

Power was thus concentrated at the top and the need even to delegate it downwards reduced. Moreover, it was all ready to be democratized at the top. The regular courts or crown-wearings, where all the lords had, not merely the right, but the obligation to assemble to give the King advice, were the origin of Parliament, or the legislature. Our political system today is barely more than a modification of Norman feudalism.

Naturally the King chose his own councillors to work with him and for him throughout the year. Originally he chose from the lords. As government became more complex, he chose also able commoners, particularly those with financial and legal qualifications. This inner council was the origin of the Government, or executive.

The word 'Parliament' was used, before the Commons existed, to describe meetings of the King, his personal councillors, the prelates, earls and barons. These early Parliaments have a direct continuity with the House of Lords, which still comprises the lords spiritual and temporal. The Commons came into existence in the thirteenth century because the King wanted to raise money over and above the traditional feudal dues. There being no law or custom to sanctify this, he felt he should explain the need for money to those who would have to pay it. The Commons first comprised elected knights of the counties. Soon the cities and towns also elected freemen. There was a period during which Parliament might still be held without the Commons. From 1311 onwards the Commons attended every Parliament. The election of the Commons had the side-effect of stimulating local government, but it was always to be subservient to the central Government.

The first members of the Commons, being concerned solely to grant the King money, no doubt kept strictly to the instructions of those who elected them—which is to say that authority was being delegated upwards. But the Commons was soon debating affairs of state (which meant that, if the King wanted to raise money, he had to listen to all their grievances and criticisms), and England was not so small that its members could journey home to consult their electors during a debate. It was inevitable that members of the Commons should be transformed from delegates into representatives—that Parliament as a whole should be 'a *deliberative* assembly of *one* nation'[10] (Burke's own italics). Since Burke's time, the power once vested in the King and his noble advisers has been completely democratized. It is now subject to universal franchise. But we have democratized it where it was, at the top.

It is enlightening to look at eighteenth-century Britain through Rousseau's eyes:

> The deputies of the people, therefore, are not and cannot be its representatives: they are merely its stewards, and can carry through no definitive acts. Every law the people has not ratified in person is null and void—is, in fact, not a law. The people of England regards itself as free; but it is grossly mistaken; it is free only during the election of members of parliament. As soon as they are elected, slavery overtakes it, and it is nothing.[11]

In Switzerland power was only gradually delegated upwards. It was not until 1848 that those elected to serve the cantons at the centre voted without instructions. Until 1848, that is to say, they constituted exactly what Burke declared the British Parliament not to be: 'a *congress* of ambassadors from different and hostile interests; which interests each must maintain, as an agent and advocate, against other agents and advocates'.[12]

If we are puzzled by the reluctance of the cantons to concede power to Berne, it is because we think of Switzerland as a country like our own. The Swiss, though patriotic, are always aware of their country as a federation. Indeed the Swiss all have three nationalities. As well as being Swiss, they take the nationalities both of their canton and their commune. Communal citizenship, like the other two, is inalienable. A family keeps its original communal citizenship even though it has lived elsewhere for generations.

The cantons retain power over most domestic matters. Some still practise in their *Landsgemeinden* a direct democracy in which all citizens may participate in debates. Referenda are common. Both the cantons and the Confederation practise collegial government. The Federal Council of seven members is elected for four years and chosen to represent different cantons and parties. It cannot be forced to resign by the legislature. Councillors tend none the less to be more loyal to one another than to their parties. The Chairmanship of the Federal Council, which carries the title of President of the Confederation, is held for only a year at a time. As Federal Councillors retire or die in office, they are replaced individually. It is virtually unknown for a Councillor not to be re-elected if willing to be. In British terms, Switzerland has had the same Government since 1848 and has yet to have a serious Government crisis.

Critics of the referendum must reckon with the fact that Switzerland, which makes the most use of it, is noted for political stability, law-abidingness, respect for liberal values, and a lack of bellicosity—this despite profound linguistic and religious divisions. Switzerland's one aberration from fullblooded democracy has been its reluctance to enfranchise women. Women were given the vote at federal level in 1971, but are still without it in two half-cantons and numerous communes. Sheer lack of space in the *Landsgemeinden* was one reason. To enfranchise women, Glaris literally tore down its old rostrum with its scaffolding and built a larger one, while Obwalden had to find a new venue. Another reason must be that the Swiss elector is called on to vote on so many Sundays in elections (for officials as well as politicians) and in referenda at federal, cantonal and communal level that it is convenient to leave someone at home to cook the lunch.

With a long Republican tradition, the Swiss are impervious to regality or pomp of any kind. Never having had a monarchical symbol, they do not experience the American need to sanctify the Constitution as a substitute. An initiative to give the Swiss Federal Supreme Court the right to examine laws for their constitutionality was rejected by a large majority in 1939. What the Swiss value above all else is the power to make their own laws.

This power they have literally retained. Under the right of initiative, any 50,000 Swiss electors may propose a constitutional amendment, which must be put to referendum. Since there is no limit on what may be added to the Constitution, 50,000 electors may propose any legislation whatever by calling it a constitutional amendment. If supported in a referendum by a majority of those voting and by majorities of those voting in a majority of the cantons, a constitutional amendment becomes law even though it has been rejected by both chambers of the legislature. Any Bill passed by both chambers must be put to referendum on the request of 30,000 electors. Its acceptance or rejection is determined by a simple majority of those voting.

In Switzerland there is no constitutional barrier between legislators and electors. It is almost immaterial whether a referendum is actually held on a Bill. It will be held if there is a demand for it. Lack of a referendum implies popular consent, as lack of a division implies parliamentary consent. The Swiss feel, as they have always felt, that the Government must obey the people. The British, until recently, felt that the people must obey the Government. It is the modification in the British attitude to Government remarked on by James Callaghan which requires a modification in British political institutions. This is not to say that Britain should adopt the Swiss Constitution—only that it should learn from it.

Membership of the EEC should enable the British to understand the Swiss better. In the EEC the British are re-learning the delegation of power upwards. The main concern of the anti-Marketeers (and of some Marketeers too) is the power of Brussels to pass laws and regulations which are valid in Britain. Nor are the British alone in feeling such anxiety. Decisions of the Council of Ministers were in fact unanimous until the summit conference in December 1974 decided that this was too restrictive and that unanimity should be required only on issues of vital national importance. Few of the Ministers in Brussels have much discretion and without the international telephone service progress would be slow. In Denmark a Select Committee of the *Folketing* (Parliament) mandates Ministers before they go to Brussels. Wherever possible, if they want to exceed their mandate they must refer back to the committee for new instructions.

No doubt the members of the EEC will learn, as the cantons did, to give their delegates more and more discretion. We are concerned, however, not with the too little discretion given to our delegates in Brussels but with the too great discretion assumed by our representatives at Westminster. I do not think our first national referendum will be our last. While the Swiss delegate more power upwards to satisfy the exigencies of modern administration, we shall delegate more downwards to satisfy the demands of modern emancipation. But, even if Switzerland and the United Kingdom came to have the same political institutions, it would be a long time before they had the same system of government. The same institutions may be worked differently. Delegation upwards or downwards is primarily an attitude of mind.

6

The *Peace News* staff would no doubt consent to vote under the Swiss system. Meanwhile, even from their own standpoint, they are wrong to scorn our own parliamentary system. It affords, not only a protection against tyranny, but a constitutional means through which to work for participatory democracy, whether in industry, in education, or in Government itself.

TERMS

We may distinguish three aspects of the working of democracy: voting; debating; initiation of subjects of debates and votes. We shall call democracy 'pure' when every citizen may take part in debates as well as vote at the end of them (even though he may not initiate subjects). The Swiss *Landsgemeinde* (or folkmoot, plural *Landsgemeinden*) and the New England town meeting are examples of pure democracy. The term 'pure' is not one of moral approbation. The most frequently cited example is ancient Athens, where perhaps half the population were slaves. An example of pure democracy in conjunction with universal franchise is afforded by our own parish meetings.

Democracy is 'direct' to the extent that citizens do their own voting and initiate subjects of debates and votes. Someone elected by citizens to do their voting for them is a 'delegate' if acting on their instructions, a 'representative' if free to decide for himself how to vote. British democracy is thus impure, indirect, and representative.

The referendum is an example of direct but not pure democracy. We may define it as:

a poll, in which every elector may vote, not preceded by a debate in which every elector may speak, on an issue.

Whether or not a poll qualifies as a referendum has nothing to do with its being taken by a show of hands or by the use of the ballot-box. Every elector is entitled to vote at a parish meeting. The only reason such a vote is not a referendum is that every elector is also entitled to speak. In practice only a few electors may choose to attend. Those who do may call for a poll of all the electors. This poll, conducted by ballot, has the look of a referendum. What disqualifies it is that all those voting in the polling-booths could have taken part in the earlier debate on the issue had they wished. Provided, however, that the essential power is with a central assembly, debates in local assemblies on national or federal measures do not disqualify the votes that follow them as referenda.

The term 'referendum' need not be restricted to polls of state and local-government electors. *The Times Educational Supplement* referred to a 'postal referendum of Leicester's 3,400 teachers',[13] conducted by a teachers' consultative committee, on the reorganization of secondary education. *The Economist* wrote that the Electrical, Electronic, Telecommunication and Plumbing Union 'holds postal referenda on major policy issues'.[14] It is even more natural to refer to the 1972 ballot of railwaymen (on whether they should strike) as a referendum. It was held under the auspices of the state—under, that is, the provisions of the Industrial Relations Act 1971. Similarly we may say that in 1974 and 1975 the Penwith District Council in Cornwall, under the Shops Act 1950, held two referenda on Sunday trading among the traders affected. The more widely the term is used, the more we shall need to speak of 'national' and 'local' referenda as we do of 'general' and 'local' elections.

It was convenient when a distinction was made between a referendum and a plebiscite. Like it or not, however, 'referendum' is established as the generic word. I shall distinguish two species: the 'constitutional referendum' and the 'plebiscite'. A constitutional referendum is provided for before the occasion of holding it arises, and is held on a Bill (or constitutional amendment) which has been debated in the legislature. Any natural-sounding usage is liable to cause confusion somewhere in the world. The Swiss will think of a constitutional referendum as one on a constitutional amendment, as distinct from a legislative referendum, or one on an ordinary Bill. 'Plebiscite' is a residual category. A plebiscite must either be an *ad hoc* referendum, one for which no constitutional provision exists, or must be held on something other than a Bill that has been debated in Parliament. In practice plebiscites usually qualify under both conditions. There were plebiscites on Napoleon III's *coup d'état*, on the unification of Italy, and on the Greek Monarchy. The 1919 peace conference proposed that seventeen national disputes should be resolved by plebiscites; eight of them were held. The 1973 Border Poll in Northern Ireland was a plebiscite: it was not held on legislation and was *ad hoc*. It was intended, however, to be the first of a ten-yearly series of Border Polls. It may be said that future Border Polls will be marginal plebiscites in that, though they will not be on legislation, there is none the less constitutional provision for them. In simple political societies it may be impossible to distinguish between constitutional referenda and plebiscites because there is no clear distinction between legislative and other decisions.

The typical unplanned plebiscite is inherently dangerous. Its timing may well be decided for demagogic ends and its result be determined by the phrasing of the question. Plebiscites have brought referenda into disrepute. It is none the less true that a plebiscite often affords the best solution of an intractable problem. Britain's first national referendum, on EEC membership, is a plebiscite. This is necessary only because we lacked provision for holding a constitutional referendum on the European Communities Bill in 1972.

Referenda (which is to say their results) may be 'binding' or 'consultative'. It is customary for constitutional referenda to be binding. A

8

plebiscite conducted within a country by its own Government is likely to be consultative. When a plebiscite is held to resolve an international dispute, the intention is usually that it should be binding.

The term 'local option' is used mainly of local referenda on the closing and opening of pubs. It has also been used in Britain of local referenda on the Sunday opening of cinemas. There is no logical reason why its application should be restricted. Switzerland might be said to have local option on capital punishment in that, though it was abolished federally in 1940, any canton could restore it in a referendum. I shall use 'local option' to refer only to pubs.

The 'initiative' is the right of a specified number or percentage of electors to introduce legislation. The term is most appropriate where the electors do not have the right to debate legislation, but it is not convenient to define it so rigorously. The initiative is worth little if the legislature can simply discuss and reject the legislation in question. Provision is usually made that initiated legislation must automatically go to referendum, or that it must go to referendum unless the legislature passes it. Subject to the provisions of the particular Constitution, an initiative may make general proposals or present a finished draft for legislation. If it makes only a general proposal, the obligation is on the legislature to convert it into legislation.

Even the Swiss have reservations about the initiative. Though it was responsible for the introduction of proportional representation (and this has proved a boon), they feel it offers scope for the trivial and the prejudiced. In the United States, where it has been widely used in the individual States, the main objection to it is that it is exploited by pressure groups. This is not to imply that legislation inspired by pressure groups must be undesirable. Often their specialist knowledge is essential to workable legislation. What is undesirable, inside or outside Parliament, is that anyone promoting legislation should be able to conceal an interest in it. The initiative lends itself to such concealment. It is better that interest groups should promote Bills in Parliament through MPs known to speak for them.

Confusion with the initiative has probably helped to bring the referendum into disrepute. Not only does an initiative often lead to a referendum. In Switzerland any 30,000 electors may require a Bill to be put to referendum, a provision which has a superficial resemblance to the initiative, though in fact it provides only a veto over legislation, not the right to introduce it.

The 'recall', associated particularly with American States, is the right of electors to dismiss representatives (whether individual ones or an entire legislature) before the next election is due. Like the referendum and initiative, the recall asserts the rights of electors *vis-à-vis* the elected. Unlike the referendum and initiative, however, it is not an example of direct democracy.

9

2
ORIGINS

REFERENDA MUST HAVE been common in primitive tribes. Pre-Roman European tribes held meetings at which only the chiefs spoke but all the freemen could 'vote' by clash of weapons or clamour. In other words, the side making the greater noise won (subject to the interpretation of the chiefs). Roman assemblies began by voting by clamour but later counted heads: 'the suggestion of individual voting, as we find it in historical time, must have come from the orderly military array, which offered itself conveniently for the purpose.'[1]

Roman referenda are the first of which we have any detailed knowledge. Qualified electors voted in person in the assemblies, but only a magistrate could put a proposal before them, and there was no opportunity for debate or amendment. Like his Italian descendant in a polling-booth, the Roman citizen could only answer Yes or No. Originally the magistrates used the procedure 'with a view not to legalizing the proposal, but to pledging the people to its practical adoption'[2] (which was a reason for putting a question to citizens individually instead of to an assembly as a whole). Gradually, however, decisions acquired the character of legislation as we understand it today.

The first Roman referenda were held before historical time, perhaps in the eighth century BC in the *comitia curiata*. This earliest of Roman assemblies was patrician in membership. It passed laws or *leges*. Our word plebiscite derives from *plebiscitum*, a resolution of the later *consilium plebis*, the Plebeian or People's Council. *Plebiscita* acquired the force of *leges* in 287 BC.

In modern times the constitutional referendum has resulted from the interaction of pure democracy and the requirements of large-scale administration. Some Swiss cantons from the thirteenth century and some American colonies from their foundation in the seventeenth exercised all the functions of government in open assembly. Swiss cantons had the *Landsgemeinde* and New England colonies the town meeting. Though there were procedural variations, citizens in both institutions generally had the right to debate laws, if not also to introduce them, so that votes on them were not referenda. For vote counting, spoken replies, shows of hands and 'divisions' into groups were all used. To this day one canton and four half-cantons retain their *Landsgemeinden*, where once a year all the citizens assemble to debate and vote. An early New England township could be an area including various villages and settlements, with all electors having the right to speak, but with religious restrictions on the franchise. Boston did not introduce a representative institution until 1822, by which time it had a population of 47,000, and it did not entirely abandon its town meeting even then. It is Switzerland and the American States which now make most use of the referendum and initiative. The *Landsgemeinde* is a derivation of the 'Thing' of the primitive German tribes, where all the ablebodied men assembled in a ring to settle disputes of law, property and boundaries, and to decide on war or peace. Germany in the Middle Ages had institutions similar to the *Landsgemeinden*. Switzerland and the American States are significant for the historical continuity of pure and direct democracy.

No less important, and also dating from the thirteenth century, were the leagues, or small federal organizations, within the territory of modern Switzerland. Those elected to serve local districts in the federal centres were strictly delegates, and in some of the leagues decisions had to be unanimous, which made for slow progress. These leagues gave us the term 'referendum', which seems to have been used first by Vulpius, who died in 1706, in his *Historica Rhaetica*, written in Latin. The Raetian Confederation (now the Grisons canton) brought together the three Raetian Leagues. The *Bundstag*, the diet of the Raetian Confederation, met only on special occasions, when matters were decided by majority votes of delegates from each *Hoch-g-ericht* in each league. The delegates were, however, bound by their instructions and had to refer back for new ones when they found their mandate exhausted. Or, as Vulpius put it, everything resolved upon by the *Bundstag* had to be transmitted to the *Hochgerichte* in the *Abschied*, for everything was done *ad referendum*.[3] The practice described did not constitute a referendum under our definition since those to whom the issue was referred could debate it as well as vote on it. In many of the leagues the local bodies did not confine themselves to voting Yes or No on a proposal but suggested an amendment, a practice which required specialist bodies to decide how the majority had voted. Since legislative matters were still usually decided at a local level, *ad referendum* issues would probably be concerned with administration, diplomacy or defence.

The pure democracy of both Switzerland and New England was a fact, not an ideal. The *Landsgemeinden* and town meetings were both based on self-interest. Both suffered from corruption, bribery in the *Landsgemeinden* being almost an institution. Some of the *Landsgemeinden* possessed and exploited subject territories. Some indeed were effectively ruled by aristocratic families. Many of the puritan

11

colonists of New England were self-consciously moral men, but despite the English Civil War their ideals were concerned more with religion and even with commerce than with politics. They could be as intolerant and as ruthless as was Cromwell at home. They were, however, worldly-wise men more or less returning to Rousseau's state of nature, and they had the precedent of democratic structure in their churches, and indeed in English civic parishes.

Massachusetts was to prove the most important of the American States in the development of the referendum. Its first permanent settlement was established at Plymouth in 1620 by the passengers on the *Mayflower*. Their only basis of Government was the Mayflower Compact, a modification of a church covenant. At first Massachusetts was a good deal less liberal than other parts of New England. At the end of the seventeenth century it persecuted witches while Connecticut developed civil and Rhode Island religious liberty. But its intolerance and persecution were, given its restricted franchise, always democratic.

For a time all the freemen of Massachusetts and Plymouth (both now Massachusetts) had a personal voice in the transaction of public business. When this was felt to be too time-consuming, delegates went to the capital carrying with them the freemen's proxies (the actual ballots they had cast in their own localities), which were all added together—though a freeman could still go to the capital to vote in person if he wished. Then delegates drew up laws and returned to their constituents to have them confirmed. Because their constituents had the right of debate in their own town meetings, there must have been a period when it was unclear whether the delegation of authority was primarily upwards or downwards. But a request on 29 May 1644 by the legislative body of Massachusetts to the elders and freemen for payment for members probably qualifies as a referendum: at least we can be confident the 'delegates' thought up the idea for themselves; and the essential function of the freemen must have been to say Yes or No.

America's main contributions to the development of the referendum have been in connection with the ratification, revision and amendment of Constitutions. An old Constitution is sanctified by tradition. A new one needs a demonstration of its acceptability to the electors. Approval by a Convention or Constituent Assembly representing the electors provides an indirect demonstration, but a Constitution will be the more secure if it also receives the direct approval of the electorate in a referendum. The need for new State Constitutions was created by the revolutionary or Independence movement.

Massachusetts was the first State to put a Constitution to referendum. The Assembly began to prepare a new form of government in 1776. A resolution in 1777 recommended the electors to 'make Choice of Men in whose Integrity and Abilities they can place the greatest Confidence. [sic] and in addition to the Common and ordinary powers of Representation vest them with full powers to form ... a Constitution of Government ...'[4] The resolution provided that copies of the new Constitution should be printed and presented to the peoples of the towns, who should vote on it. It was to become valid only if approved by two-thirds of those voting. The Constitution duly drawn up the legislature was put to referendum in 1778. Because it had been drawn up by the Assembly and not by a special constitutional Convention, because it lacked a Bill of Rights, and for other reasons, it was rejected by a majority of five to one. The town meetings debated it before voting on it, and some proposed detailed amendments. But this need not prevent us from calling the poll a referendum: essentially the Constitution was handed down by the legislature for the people to accept or reject—and this was itself a reason it was rejected. This referendum was a plebiscite: though held under the auspices of the existing Assembly, no provision existed for it before the occasion for holding it arose. The next time the Assembly proceeded differently. It first established in a plebiscite in 1779 that a constitutional Convention should be held. The second Constitution was subsequently approved by a two-thirds majority in a plebiscite in 1780. This was the first State Constitution to be approved in a referendum and is the oldest still in force.

But for the military exigencies of the time, plebiscites might have been held on other new State Constitutions before 1778—particularly on that of Pennsylvania, where French (Rousseauesque) thought was influential. The Maryland Constitution of 1776 allowed the legislature to amend the Constitution if it passed the necessary Bill three months before an election and confirmed it during the first session afterwards —which obliged the legislature to obtain a mandate. The Georgia Constitution of 1777 provided for a Convention on the signature of majorities of electors in a majority of the counties—an anticipation of the initiative rather than of the referendum.

The only other State actually to submit a Constitution to referendum during the revolutionary period was New Hampshire. Like the electors of Massachusetts, those of New Hampshire rejected the first submitted to them, in 1779, and accepted the second, in 1783. This second Constitution, inaugurated in 1784, provided for a Convention after seven years, its recommendations for amending the Constitution to be subject to approval in a referendum by two-thirds of those voting. This provision has foresight enough to qualify as a constitutional referendum, despite its time restriction. After the revolutionary period, it became customary to hold referenda on new State Constitutions: there might be a referendum on whether there should be a Convention, on the Convention's proposals, or on both. This custom was respected until

13

the end of the nineteenth century, when certain Southern States drew up Constitutions designed to disfranchise the blacks.

So far we have been concerned with the creation of new or the substantial revision of existing Constitutions. The Connecticut Constitution of 1818 was the first to provide for its own amendment, without restriction in time, by approval of the legislature and also of the electorate in a referendum: the House of Representatives could propose a constitutional amendment by a simple majority; if after the next election both Houses passed it by two-thirds majorities, it was to be put to referendum and become law if supported by simple majorities of those voting in the town meetings. Other State Constitutions incorporated the same principle with variations. Maine in 1819 was the first State to abandon the requirement that a constitutional amendment be passed in two successive legislatures—to abandon, that is, the requirement for an election as well as a referendum. Here we have the constitutional referendum in its purest form.

American practice had been influenced by French thought. French thought was in turn influenced by American practice. The 1793 Girondin Constitution, which in the event was never adopted, was the systematic union of Rousseauesque philosophy and New England experience. The National Convention regarded the Constitution as the social contract (though it is interesting that the Girondin Constitution uses the term 'social compact' or *pacte sociale*).[5] It voted to establish the New England principle: *'La Convention nationale declare qu'il ne peut y avoir de Constitution que lorsque'elle est acceptée par le peuple.'*[6] The local primary assemblies of both the Girondin and the actual 1793 Constitutions were consciously related to the town meetings. In the Girondin Constitution the intricate relations between the primary assemblies and the legislature could be described as an attempt to establish pure democracy on a national scale.

After the overthrow of the Girondins in 1793, the National Convention adopted a Jacobin Constitution. British constitutional authorities have seen it as a writ for anarchy. It was similar to the Girondin Constitution, but, as seen by French authorities, *'plus brève, plus cohérente, plus pratique'*.[7] It provided for universal suffrage and the constitutional referendum on all Bills (but not decrees). A Bill had to be distributed in all the communes. It became law forty days later unless there were objections to it by a tenth of the primary assemblies in each of half the Departments plus one, when the primary assemblies had to be convoked (for the purpose of voting on it). In the primary assemblies *'Les suffrages sur les lois sont donnés par "oui"' et par "non".'*[8] A tenth of the primary assemblies in half the Departments plus one could also demand a National Convention for the revision of the Constitution. Though accepted both by the National Convention and by the people in a plebiscite based on universal male suffrage, the

1793 Constitution was never worked.

The French Revolution's assertion of popular sovereignty, not only established in Europe the principle that a new Constitution should be approved by the people, but led to a spate of plebiscites on self-determination. Surprisingly a plebiscite on self-determination had been held nearly two and a half centuries earlier. Before the French Revolution, sovereignty was generally determined by the inheritance or marriage of the reigning monarch, by conquest, or by barter, though the nobles and even the common people were capable of protesting when their territories were ceded to a ruler to whom they took exception. The first deliberate use of self-determination was made defensively by Francis i of France. Defeated in battle, he ceded Burgundy to the Holy Roman Emperor, Charles v, by the Treaty of Madrid in 1526. The next year he successfully appealed to the Burgundian estates (Parliament) to invalidate the cession. Francis's son and successor, Henry ii of France, used the principle of self-determination acquisitively in 1552 when, after occupying Toul, Metz and Verdun more or less painlessly, he had votes of the people taken in them before annexing them. Henry appears to have ordered the first plebiscite in medieval or modern history, and the last before the French Revolution.

The democratic practices of the French Revolution were less idealistic than their theory. The voting for the 1793 Constitution, accepted by 1,801,918 votes to 11,610, is held not to have been free. No serious criticism is made of the plebiscite on the 1795 Constitution, though this was also accepted by 1,057,390 votes to 49,997. In the plebiscite on the 1799 Constitution, acceptance was by 3,000,000 votes to 1,500. This time, instead of voting in the primary assemblies, electors were required to sign separate registers in the capitals. The events of the French Revolution had not disposed citizens to sign the anti register, which was in effect a list of the Government's opponents. Napoleon was appointed Consul for life in 1802 by the same method.

These domestic plebiscites had been preceded by others in foreign territories on union with France. In the early years of the French Revolution the doctrine of self-determination, which was held to follow inevitably from that of popular sovereignty, was treated with respect. The Constituent Assembly in 1790 renounced all wars of conquest, and the declaration was included in the 1791 Constitution. For two years, from 1789 to 1791, the Assembly resisted demands to annex Avignon and Comtat Venaissin, two pieces of Papal territory forming an enclave within France, despite requests from both their own inhabitants and the French citizenry, and despite the pretext afforded by the outbreak of civil war within them. When, during this civil war, many of the communes voted for union with France, the Assembly feared coercion and still declined to annex them, but sent three mediators to negotiate an end to the civil war and resolve the territories' future.

A plebiscite was organized in 1791. Those entitled to vote were men other than domestic servants, of twenty-five or over, who paid taxes of about 30 cents a year. They were summoned by town crier or placards the day before the voting. On the day itself a meeting was held in the chief church of the commune. After an address the presiding officer, who might be the mayor or the eldest citizen, put the question in his own words. One or two communes seem to have voted by ballot. In most the electors divided: those for union with France remained in the body of the church; those for the *status quo* under the Pope moved into the chapel; or *vice versa*. The addresses may have emphasized the advantages of union with France. Despite the arguably intimidating presence of French troops to attempt to keep order, there were serious disturbances affecting the fairness of voting. None the less the French seem to have wanted to be fair, and the result, in favour of union with France, seems to have represented majority opinion.

The plebiscites in which Savoy, in 1792, and Nice, in 1793, voted for union with France also seem to have been essentially fair. When, however, the Belgians showed themselves disinterested in union, the degeneration, in December 1792, was immediate: the franchise was limited to those in sympathy with the Revolution, the voting was manipulated, and electors were coerced. That was the end of idealism, though Napoleon on occasion modified force with tact. The last of these French plebiscites in conquered territories was in Switzerland in 1802. Between 1815 and 1848 the restoration of the old order suppressed the doctrines of popular sovereignty and self-determination. The revolutions in 1848 once more asserted them throughout Europe, and particularly in Italy and Schleswig-Holstein.

After occupying Switzerland, the French had imposed a new Constitution, that of the One and Indivisible Helvetic Republic of 1798. Until this time, not only were delegates to the Diet of the Swiss Confederation bound by instructions from the cantons, but as a general rule decisions were unanimous. The Helvetic Republic gave Switzerland a unitary state with representative government. French dictation was resented, but the Swiss were divided on the federal issue, and in the 'patrician' cantons the invaders were welcomed. There was civil war and a series of unworkable Constitutions, with Napoleon conceding some cantonal sovereignty. It was the fifth Constitution which in 1802 was put to a plebiscite of all the men over twenty. This was the first time the Swiss had voted on a Constitution. The public-register system of voting was used: only 72,453 voted in favour; 92,423 voted against; while 167,172 refrained from voting. Despite the majority against, the abstainers were held to have expressed tacit approval, and the Constitution was adopted.

By the qualification of experience, the Swiss were entitled to give the French lessons in democracy. They resented having a Constitution imposed upon them by foreigners in the name of the principles of the French Revolution when their own 'form of government put the sovereign power so exclusively in the hands of the people'.[9] The good that came out of the French occupation was the establishment of the subject territories within the Swiss Confederation as independent cantons. Despite themselves, the Swiss were influenced by French theory. We have said that Swiss democracy was a fact, not an ideal—witness the lack of embarrassment over the subject territories. It was only in the nineteenth century, using the vocabulary of the French Revolution, that the Swiss began to believe in and take pride in their distinctive form of democracy.

A degree of centralisation survived the fall of Napoleon. The years after 1815, in Switzerland as elsewhere in Europe, were reactionary. It was the French Revolution of 1830 which inspired an irresistible demand for democratic rights in Switzerland. The federal Diet conceded in the same year the right of the cantons to revise their Constitutions. Between 1830 and 1834 twenty Constitutions were revised, their new versions being submitted to the peoples of their cantons for ratification. The main features of the new Constitutions were universal male suffrage and the constitutional 'veto'. Before 1830 the cantons (except those that retained their *Landsgemeinden*) had experienced representative government. In varying degrees they were to re-establish pure and develop direct democracy.

The first canton to adopt the constitutional veto was St Gall in March 1831: laws had to be promulgated; fifty citizens in a commune could convoke a communal assembly to debate a law and vote on it; a majority of all the citizens voting in their communal assemblies could reject a law, except that non-voters were counted as supporters. The term 'veto' referred to this presumption in favour of passing a law. The essential power was now in the cantons. We shall therefore allow that St Gall's veto was the first modern constitutional referendum on ordinary legislation, though the debates in the communes and the voting conditions make its qualification marginal. The Valais in 1839 introduced what may be called the compulsory veto. All laws (and indeed all military capitulations, financial decrees, and acts of naturalization) had to be voted on in the primary assemblies. Still no law could be rejected except by an absolute majority of the registered electors. This provision was abolished in 1844. Henceforth all laws had simply to be approved by a majority of those voting in the communal assemblies. It was in 1844 therefore that the veto was converted into a pure constitutional referendum on ordinary legislation. The next year Vaud adopted the initiative.

The federal Constitution of 1848 (adopted in a referendum) established a Government as distinct from a congress of ambassadors, with a bicameral legislature based on that of the United States, one chamber representing the cantons. It provided for compulsory referenda on constitutional amendments: an amendment would be adopted if accepted by a majority of those voting and by majorities of those voting in a majority of the cantons. It provided also for 50,000 electors to initiate a revision of the Constitution. There was no provision for either the referendum or the initiative on ordinary legislation.

During the 1860s there was a further revulsion against representative government in the cantons. Rural-Basle provided in May 1863 that 'No law or important decree can come into force without having been approved by the referendum; and, furthermore, any 1,500 electors have the right of provoking a vote of the people at any time on the question of the repeal or amendment of a law in force.'[10] A spate of constitutional revisions in other cantons introduced a variety of forms of the referendum and initiative, and inevitably the influence extended to the federal Government.

In 1874 a revised federal Constitution (adopted in a referendum) provided for the referendum on ordinary legislation: any 30,000 electors or eight cantons could demand a referendum on a Bill, its acceptance or rejection being determined by a simple majority of those voting. A dispute about whether the initiative introduced in 1848 applied only to total revisions of the Constitution was resolved in 1891: the right of 50,000 electors to initiate partial revisions (constitutional amendments) was specifically established. The federal Constitution still does not provide for the initiative for ordinary legislation. Since, however, there is no restriction on what may be added to the Constitution, any 50,000 electors may initiate any legislation by calling it a constitutional amendment. This explains why the Swiss Constitution contains a clause on the slaughter of animals.

The United States followed the Swiss example. During the nineteenth century it had preserved the referendum tradition mainly in local option in liquor control in counties and cities. Beginning with South Dakota in 1898, twenty-two States adopted the constitutional referendum on ordinary legislation. Most of them also adopted the initiative for ordinary legislation, and some the initiative for constitutional amendments. The referendum and initiative were seen by the progressive parties as a means of passing responsible radical legislation despite corrupt boss-controlled legislatures. The States with the referendum are mainly in the West, but they include Maine and Massachusetts in the East. Massachusetts adopted it only in 1918.

The federal Constitution of the United States contains no provision for the referendum. Nor has there ever been a federal referendum. The American War of Independence was fought, not for the French principle of popular sovereignty, but for the British principle of no taxation without representation. The Founding Fathers rejected both French influence and the indigenous tradition of the town meeting.

18

They drew up a Constitution that has been described as more monarchical than the British and as aristocratic. The American people enjoy only qualified representative government. They vote for electoral colleges, which vote for a President on their behalf. None the less it was from the United States that the temperance movement brought advocacy of the referendum to Britain.

3
LOCAL REFERENDA

LOCAL OPTION

THE LOCAL POLITICAL unit under the Normans was the manor. But the early ecclesiastical parishes continued to discuss civil matters. Indeed parishes were not ecclesiastical even in origin. In the south the church had adopted the Anglo-Saxon township as the district of the parish priest. It became general practice for the parson to require the parish landowners to meet the cost of maintaining the church. Partly inspired by the principle of no taxation without representation, parish meetings were held to discuss income and expenditure. Attendance at these meetings, held not less than once a year, was extended, with the duty to make contributions, from the land-owners of a parish to all its inhabitants.

Parish meetings concerned themselves more and more with civil matters in the thirteenth and fourteenth centuries. With the dissolution of the monasteries under Henry VIII, the parishes were used for the administration of the Poor Law and established as civil units. The ecclesiastical origin of the parish meeting made it perfectly democratic: under the chairmanship of the parson 'Even the lord of the manor himself and his underlings were here on a par with the poorer members of the Christian community.'[1] The parish meeting was traditionally held in the vestry and came to be called the vestry. In the towns and larger rural parishes open vestries gave way to select vestries, standing committees recruited by co-option and representative of vested interests. There were other abuses too. But many of the smaller rural parishes have preserved a genuine direct democracy to this day.

Vestries became involved in an early exercise in local option on the closing of pubs. Under the influence of the Evangelical Movement, and in particular of a Royal Proclamation against vice and immorality issued at the instigation of Wilberforce in 1787, benches of magistrates exercised a strict control over pubs—though only for about six years. They introduced early closing and Sunday closing, refused new licences and withdrew existing ones. In many counties the consent of the 'principal inhabitants in vestry assembled' became a condition of the granting of new licences. Some counties even called the principal inhabitants into council to pronounce on the renewal of existing licences. 'It is significant,' wrote the Webbs, 'that the Justices of the Peace of the latter part of the eighteenth century—frequently cited as the most oligarchical and autocratic of governing authorities—habitually made use of local option or local veto in their administration of the Liquor Laws.'[2] This is true despite the fact that the vestries they were consulting were select rather than open.

Local option on a wide franchise originated independently in the United States. The Georgian legislature in 1833 gave local courts in two counties the right to grant or withhold licences. Since in American practice the members of the courts were elected, this constituted indirect local option. Soon Statutes in various States permitted the electorates in local political units—usually counties, but sometimes cities, towns, villages, and even districts of a city—to vote directly on both on-licences and off-licences. Local option led to State Prohibition in Maine in 1851 and in a further twelve States before the outbreak of the Civil War in 1861.

The United Kingdom Alliance for the Suppression of the Traffic in all Intoxicating Liquors, founded in 1853, first advocated national Prohibition by a single Act of Parliament. Impressed by American experience, it adopted a policy of local option in 1857, and in 1864 Wilfred (later Sir Wilfred) Lawson introduced the Permissive Bill. Although 'permissive' did not have its present connotations, the Alliance suffered from the choice of title and was at pains to explain that the permission granted was to ratepayers to prohibit the sale of drink. Lawson's fear that his Bill might be rejected by the Lords proved wildly optimistic: it was rejected by the Commons itself by 292 votes to 35. (The term 'local option' was coined later, and has been attributed to Gladstone.) Lawson persisted in introducing Bills and resolutions on local option. A resolution was finally carried in 1880, after a Liberal victory in the general election, by 229 votes to 203.

Local option had appeared in a Liberal Government Bill, in relation to additional licences, in 1871. It had lost the Liberals by-elections and the general election of 1874. The 150 Liberal candidates who were local optionists had done particularly badly. After broken promises by both parties, attempts by the Conservatives to introduce local option in 1888 and 1890 were both dropped because of temperance opposition to compensation for the suppression of licences. In 1893 the Liberals introduced an unsuccessful Bill providing for local option without compensation. This was the year in which the Liberals finally adopted local option as official policy, beginning the era of such improbable temperance advocates as Asquith and Winston Churchill. Churchill actually presided over the United Kingdom Alliance's Annual Meeting in 1907. It was poetic justice when in 1922 he was defeated at Dundee by Edwin Scrymgeor, who described himself as Britain's first Prohibition candidate.

The Conservatives solved the compensation problem in the 1904 Licensing Act. This provided for compensation from a fund raised by a levy on the trade. The Liberals incorporated this principle in their 1908 Licensing Bill, providing for local option on the reduction of pubs. The rejection of this Bill by the Lords was one of the causes of the Parliament Act 1911 and of the first serious talk of a national referendum. Local option lost the Liberals more support at by-elections and was discredited as a realistic policy by the First World War. Lloyd George declared himself ready in 1915 to take a pledge never to touch alcohol legislation again. By this time, however, the temperance lobby had been appeased with the passing of the Temperance (Scotland) Act 1913.

This provided for polls in small burghs, the wards of large burghs, and the parishes of counties to decide whether the licensed trade should carry on as it was; or the number of pubs should be reduced by 25 per cent; or all pubs and retail licences should be abolished. No Licence would be carried if 55 per cent of those voting favoured it and if they constituted 35 per cent of the registered voters. Limitation would be carried by a bare majority of the voters provided again that those in favour constituted 35 per cent of the registered electors. If No Licence was not carried, votes in favour of it would be taken instead as favouring Limitation. The well-worked-out technical details favoured the wets. A poll was to be taken on a requisition signed by a tenth of the voters in an area. Three years had to elapse between polls in any one area.

The first polls under the Act were held in November and December 1920 (there being none during either of the World Wars). Scotland was divided into 1,215 areas, of which 308 were without pubs in the first place. Of the 907 areas with pubs, only 584 held polls at all, only 40 of these voted for No Licence, and only another 35 for Limitation. (These were the figures after a few of the polls had been declared void and new ones held—to the benefit of the wets.) The best the temperance movement achieved was thirty-eight dry areas and thirty-six with limiting resolutions. After the 1920s, polls were requisitioned mainly for the purpose of restoring licences. There are now sixteen No Licence areas and fifteen with limiting resolutions.

The provisions of the 1913 Act were re-enacted in the Licensing (Scotland) Act 1959. Polls have continued to be held, nineteen from 1962 to 1967, seven from 1968 to 1974. Despite the disappearance of the burgh in local-government reform in 1974, the old areas were retained for the purpose of the temperance polls. This was partly because of the problem of voting No Change in areas formerly half wet and half dry, partly because of the imminence of the Clayson Report, which in the event recommended the abolition of the Scottish temperance polls.[3] No decision has yet been taken on this recommendation.

Between the wars various Bills sought to introduce local option in other parts of the United Kingdom. Nothing came of them. Before the Second World War local option ceased to be an issue. But there was to be a dénouement. Welsh Sunday closing had been introduced in 1881, the result of a militant minority and a restricted franchise. It was planned to abolish it in the 1961 Licensing Act, if only because a large proportion of adult Welsh males belonged to Sunday drinking clubs. In the event the Government deferred to outraged nonconformity to the extent of allowing local option on Welsh Sunday closing on the basis of counties and county boroughs. The temperance movement had envisaged local option as creeping Prohibition. It had never believed in democracy for its own sake—and had not hesitated to oppose licences in Scottish areas that voted wet. It was the biter bit.

In the first polls in 1961 all four county boroughs and five of the thirteen counties went wet. The provisions of the 1961 Act (re-enacted in the Licensing Act 1964) allowed polls to be held only every seven years and only on requisitions signed by 500 electors. A further three counties went wet in 1968, leaving only five dry (or drinking in clubs). With local-government reorganization in 1974, the bad decision was taken to base future polls (the next in November of 1975) on the thirty-seven new districts and not on the eight new large counties. Small units favour the dries. The best solution would have been a single poll for the whole of Wales. This would have given Wales a sensible licensing system without exposing the Westminster Government to the charge of imperialism.

PUBLIC LIBRARIES

The British ruling classes had none of the American enthusiasm for direct democracy: they feared referenda even at a local level and on a restricted franchise.[4] After the French Revolution they feared popular education no less than popular government. After 1848, however, they were able to regard revolution as a continental phenomenon. They set about abolishing the 'taxes on knowledge' which had restricted newspaper sales; and in the Public Libraries Act 1850 they provided that the halfpenny rates, which since 1845 it had been possible to devote to a local museum, could be devoted alternatively or additionally to a (free) public library.

The early local option exercised by the vestries was pure democracy. Provision for Britain's first local referenda was passed quietly in this Public Libraries Act: an English or Welsh municipal council with a population of 10,000 or more could hold a poll of ratepayers on the adoption of the Act; a two-thirds majority of the votes cast was needed to put the Act into operation. Joseph Hume and John Bright, while supporting the Bill, had asked that its adoption be conditional on the approval of a majority of the ratepayers.

23

The Act was extended to Scotland and Ireland in 1853. An Act of 1854 empowered Scottish library authorities to spend a penny instead of a halfpenny rate on a library. It also provided for the adoption of the Act, by two-thirds of those voting, at a public meeting of £10 householders, though a poll might be demanded by any five electors present. An Act of 1855 gave Ireland a penny rate and the right of adoption by two-thirds of those voting at a public meeting of householders, but made no provision for a poll.

The Public Libraries Act 1855 gave England and Wales a penny rate and introduced a public-meeting procedure (with poll provision in parishes). Under this Act, the population limit was reduced from 10,000 to 5,000, and library authorities could be, not only municipal boroughs, but improvement boards or commissions and parish vestries or groups of vestries. An amending Act of 1866, relating to England, Wales and Scotland, removed the population limit, substituted a simple for a two-thirds majority at a public meeting, and abolished existing provision for polls. An Act of 1867 defined the Scottish library authorities in detail. A general Act of 1877 restored polls in England, Wales, Scotland and Ireland. (Ireland lost provision for polls from 1890 to 1894.)

From 1887 adoption by public meeting was limited in Scotland to authorities with not more than 3,000 householders: larger authorities could adopt only by poll. From 1890 England and Wales required adoption by poll in all authorities except parishes. A consolidating Act of 1892 further defined library authorities in England and Wales, leaving 'in an unsatisfactory state ... the procedure for adoption, which was cumbersome, expensive, and uncertain in its results'.[5] The next year English urban authorities were empowered to adopt without a poll— that is, by a simple council resolution. This power was extended to Scottish burghs in 1894. The Education (Scotland) Act 1918 effectively freed Scottish county authorities from the restriction of the penny rate. The Public Libraries Act 1919 did the same for all English authorities and conferred on county councils the power of adoption in areas where the Public Libraries Acts had not already been adopted (and by agreement in areas where they had). The non-county Scottish authorities had their rate limit raised to threepence in 1920 and abolished in 1955. Scottish provision for polls and meetings was repealed by an Act of 1973.

The Local Government Act 1894 was interpreted to mean that in every rural parish in England and Wales the parish meeting had the exclusive power of adopting the Public Libraries Act, save that a single elector at a meeting could demand a poll. After the Public Libraries Act 1919 a parish could exercise this power only if its area had not been adopted by the county. The provisions for the 1894 Act were superseded by the Local Government Act 1933, providing for a poll to be taken by ballot as if it were a poll for the election of parish councillors: a poll could be demanded at a parish meeting 'on any question arising thereat',[6] including the adoption of the Public Libraries Acts, if the person presiding consented or the demand was made by not less than five or a third of the electors present, whichever was the less. These provisions have been re-enacted virtually unchanged in the Local Government Act 1972, but we may regard them as doubly academic, since, not only do parish polls not qualify as referenda, but the Public Libraries and Museums Act 1964, which encouraged larger library authorities, deprived parishes of the power of adoption.

The library referenda were important, if at all, only in the nineteenth century. No doubt the ruling classes preferred public libraries to public houses as the first subject of local referenda because they were less exciting. Few of the enfranchised bothered to vote in the library referenda; and the disfranchised working classes, though widely canvassed, raised little in the way of subscriptions for the public-library movement.

The establishment of public libraries was attributable mainly to members of the upper and upper-middle classes (and to professional librarians). Their motives were predominantly philanthropic, though the mill-owners among them wanted better-educated workers and in the late nineteenth century there was recognition of the need to 'educate our masters'. The low polls in the referenda enabled nineteenth-century do-gooders to exploit apathy much as twentieth-century trade-union militants have done. Ironically the first statutory use of the referendum was responsible for one of the most paternalistic developments in British history.

PRIVATE BILLS

Private Bills (to be distinguished from Private Members' Bills) are concerned with matters of local or specialized interest. They originated in the right of the subject to petition the Crown for the redress of personal grievances. Though little reported in the national press, they require a lot of work in Committee both in the Commons and the Lords. Many are promoted by local authorities to acquire sanction for projects affecting only their own areas. The promotion of Private Bills by local authorities was brought under central control during the second half of the nineteenth century. A digression is necessary to understand how.

The Local Government Act 1858 provided for its own adoption in places with a known boundary (with certain exceptions) by a resolution passed at a meeting of the owners and ratepayers. Any owner or ratepayer at the meeting could, however, require the issue to be resolved instead by a poll of the owners and ratepayers. Adoptive Acts (Public Libraries Acts afford other examples) were a feature of local-government legislation in the nineteenth and earlier twentieth centuries. They are a somewhat cumbersome method of granting permissive powers—of entitling local authorities to establish libraries or take public-health measures without obliging them to do so. The Local Government Act 1858, which applied only to England and Wales, was repealed by the Public Health Act 1875. The local referenda it provided for on its own adoption constitute a small category on their own.

The Borough Funds Act 1872, passed to rectify a court ruling in 1871 that the promotion or opposition of Bills could not be financed from the borough fund, provided that in England and Wales the consent of the owners and ratepayers should be expressed by the poll procedure of the 1858 Act. Under the Borough Funds Act 1903 a borough or urban district council in England or Wales (unless retaining powers from a special Act) had to advertise its intention to promote a Private Bill and call a public meeting to consider it. Whatever the decision of the meeting, a poll could be demanded by a hundred electors or one-twentieth of the total electors, whichever was the less. If the decision was against the proposal, the council itself could demand a poll. This Act had the effect of substituting a poll of the local-government electors for one of the house owners and ratepayers.

A parish poll is not a referendum because the electors could all have spoken in the debate at the parish meeting had they wished. In principle a similar relation existed between meetings and polls in the larger local-authority districts involved in the referenda on public libraries, Private Bills, and the Sunday opening of cinemas. In practice the numbers involved meant that not all who wished to could speak at the meetings. Hence the subsequent polls must be regarded as referenda. These meetings did not have the sites, let alone the tradition and organization, of the *Landsgemeinden*. Sir Herbert (later Lord) Samuel, describing the Private Bill meetings when proposing that a similar procedure be adopted in the Sunday Entertainments Bill 1932, made them sound perfunctory:

> If in any area it is proposed that Sunday opening should be permitted, a poll is to be taken of the electors, but the present Statutes provide that it is unnecessary to take a poll if there is no opposition, and in order to ascertain whether there is opposition or not a public meeting has to be held, a town's meeting presided over by the Lord Mayor or the Mayor as the case may be. That, of course, is not a good way of arriving at a decision in a matter such as this. To call a meeting which, perhaps, 500,000 people would be entitled to attend, and to expect them to debate seriously a question of this kind, and arrive at a reasoned conclusion, is not a practicable proposal; but that is not what, in fact, takes place. At the present time when a question arises as to whether a Private Bill should be

promoted in Parliament for dealing with some local matter a public meeting is called, and, if it be obvious that there are 100 objectors, then immediately a poll is ordered without further debate. That is what will take place in this case. We cannot eliminate the public meeting altogether, because that would mean that the district would have to go to the expense of a poll even if there were no opposition; but it is not intended or expected that a public meeting is to arrive at a reasoned conclusion; it will only provide an opportunity for it to be made clear to the local authority whether there are 100 objectors in the town, and if so, a poll must be ordered straight away.[7]

The Borough of Hove sought to promote a Private Bill in January 1966. The resolution put to the public meeting was:

That the electors of the Borough of Hove hereby approve the promotion by the Council of that borough of Part III (Works) of the Hove Corporation Bill, 1966, in so far as it relates to Work No. 1 (an improvement of Kingsway from St. John's Road to the eastern boundary of the borough including lowering a part of Adelaide Crescent on its south side) and Work No. 2 (a new street including a junction with Work No. 1 from the west side to the east side of Adelaide Crescent) together with so much of the preamble and of the other provisions of the Bill as relates or is ancillary to those provisions.

The voting in the subsequent poll was:

In favour of the resolution	2,787
Against the resolution	4,970
Majority against	2,183
Turnout	13.4 per cent
Cost of poll	£446 10s 5d

The Local Government (County Borough and Adjustments) Act 1926 excepted from the public-meeting-poll procedure Bills to constitute boroughs or county boroughs or to extend the areas of county boroughs. The public-meeting-poll provisions of the Borough Funds Act 1903, as amended by the 1926 Act, were re-enacted in the Local Government Act 1933. They were not re-enacted in the Local Government Act 1972 and lapsed, with local-government re-organization, on 1 April 1974.

SUNDAY CINEMAS
The Sunday Observance Act 1780 prohibited (in England and Wales) any public entertainment, amusement or debate to which admission was by the payment of money or tickets sold for money. In the early

27

twentieth century, cinemas in many parts of the country none the less opened on Sundays, often giving the proceeds to charity. After the passing of the Cinematograph Act 1909, licences had to be obtained from local authorities to use premises for cinematograph exhibitions. Many of the local licensing authorities granted licences for Sunday performances. In 1931 the High Court ruled that, in view of the provisions of the 1780 Act, a licensing authority had no power to grant such permission.

A solution was afforded by the Sunday Entertainments Act 1932, which introduced a procedure to permit the Sunday opening of cinemas if local opinion expressed itself in favour. The local authority had to submit a draft order to the Home Secretary for approval by both Houses of Parliament. A borough, urban or rural district council was required to advertise locally its intention of submitting a draft order. In a borough or urban district, a public meeting of local-government electors was held to consider the proposal. Again the decision of the meeting was final unless a hundred electors or a twentieth of the electorate, or, in the event of rejection, the council itself, called for a poll.

The Act did not apply to Scotland or Northern Ireland. Resisting an amendment to exclude Wales from the Bill, Oliver Stanley, Under-Secretary of State at the Home Office, pointed out that it would remain possible for a Welsh local authority to exercise 'local option' by using the Private Bill procedure. The public meeting and the poll would be exactly the same as under the Sunday Entertainments Bill: 'All that we do is to cut out the expensive, cumbersome and quite unnecessary Committee Stage in the House of Commons ...'[8]

The public meetings and polls were brought to an end by the Sunday Cinema Act 1972. Local licensing authorities in England and Wales may now allow cinemas to open on Sundays subject to normal licensing conditions.

One of these past local referenda must be examined in detail to understand the character of the public meeting and the ensuing campaign. I have chosen one from the spate of referenda held on the Sunday opening of cinemas just after the Second World War. Many towns had availed themselves of powers under Defence Regulation 42B (passed in 1939) to allow cinemas to open on Sundays even though they had never held referenda. A taste for Sunday cinema-going had been acquired. The war had affected many Sunday practices and generally increased permissiveness. In most of the post-war referenda it was predictable that a poll would favour Sunday opening. One town where the result was uncertain was Halifax.

During the war Halifax Town Council obtained powers under Defence Regulation 42B to allow Sunday opening, but could not come to terms with the cinematograph exhibitors over the proportion of gross profits to be given to charity. When Halifax's referendum was held in February 1947, these powers were still operative and were not due to expire until the December. Halifax could have had Sunday opening at the time without a referendum, but it would not have been permanent.

At the end of a lengthy debate on 4 December 1946, the Halifax Town Council resolved to call a public meeting to decide whether application should be made for powers to allow the Sunday opening of cinemas under the Sunday Entertainments Act 1932. It was evident that more councillors voted for the public meeting—and by implication for a referendum—than favoured Sunday opening.

The Council had acted in response to a letter from the Cinematograph Exhibitors' Association. The churches opposed Sunday opening: a number combined to form the Halifax Citizens' Sunday Defence Committee, which raised a few hundred pounds, spent mainly on posters, leaflets and newspaper advertising. The Halifax Secular Society declared its support for Sunday cinemas. Both sides canvassed. The Defence Committee developed an efficient ward organization.

The Defence Committee's advertising declared that even those who abstained from voting would be ranging themselves with atheists and anti-religionists. A correspondence in the *Courier and Guardian* examined whether it was even possible for a freethinker to hold moral values. Though predominantly Christian, the opponents also made use of secular arguments. Sunday was a day not merely of worship but of rest. It preserved family life. It encouraged people to think for themselves and find their own amusements. Much was made of the fact that the initiative for Sunday opening came from the cinema industry, described by the Rev. Ralph Rumney at the public meeting as 'an octopus stretching out from Hollywood, with its tentacles over every town and village'.[9]

Supporters of Sunday opening stressed libertarian arguments. Sunday opening would allow people to make up their own minds. Those who wanted to go to the cinema could. The rest need not. Workers on shift work or taking evening classes might have no opportunity to go to the cinema except on Sunday. People could go to church in the morning and to the cinema in the afternoon or evening. Why not cinemas when golf, bowls, tennis and the wireless were allowed? Some supporters did not hesitate to present themselves as defenders of the English Sunday: cinemas would keep grown-ups out of the pubs and children off the streets.

The climax of the debate was of course the public meeting, held in the Victoria Hall on Wednesday 15 January 1947. With the meeting due to start at 7.30 p.m., the doors were opened at 7 p.m. A queue of 400 had already assembled. The doors closed at 7.20. Rather more than 2,000 had gained entrance. Nearly as many were turned away.

The Mayor, Councillor C. H. Lucas, presided. The Town Clerk, Mr W. Usher, explained the purpose of the meeting. The Mayor put the resolution in favour of seeking powers to allow Sunday cinemas, explained that forms for the requisition of a referendum would be available at the close of the meeting and thereafter from the Town Clerk's office, and opened the debate. Those intending to speak had been asked to sit in the front row. Each speaker was asked to give his or her name and address and invited to a dais to speak into a microphone. After the fifteenth speech, the Mayor imposed a four-minute limit on further speeches. Twenty-seven speeches were made, fourteen in favour of Sunday opening and thirteen against. The *Courier and Guardian* reported that despite an inevitable 'unruly element' there was no rowdiness and 'the large company was good-humoured as well as lively in its partisanship'.[10]

At the end of the debate the Ayes and Noes were asked to stand in turn and were counted by checkers each responsible for a number of rows. The count was 673 for Sunday cinemas and 1,039 against. The meeting closed at 10 p.m.

A victory for the antis at a public meeting is of no great account. The antis tend to be keener: not only do they attend meetings in greater numbers; they get there sooner and head the queue, with the result that a greater proportion of their opponents are left outside when the doors are closed. If bookmakers had made a practice of taking bets on poll results in those days, they would have made Sunday opening odds on despite the vote at the meeting.

The Mayor duly received in writing, on Monday 20 January, a requisition signed by more than a hundred electors asking for a poll under the Sunday Entertainments Act on the question of obtaining an Order authorizing Sunday cinema shows in Halifax. It was decided to hold the poll on Thursday 6 February, with voting from 12 noon to 8 p.m.

On polling day Halifax was snowbound, with deep drifts in higher parts. The inhabitants of the remoter cottages were cut off.

The voting was:

For Sunday cinemas	9,935
Against Sunday cinemas	8,458
Majority for Sunday cinemas	1,477

Turnout 25.1 per cent

In the weather conditions a 25 per cent poll was high. The Cinemas Association had the better organization on the day, with eleven loud-speaker vans and a fleet of cars. But it could be that the weather deterred the elderly from going to the poll and determined the result.

Rather than wait until a draft Order had been submitted to the Home Secretary and referred by him to both Houses of Parliament, the Town Council now availed itself of its powers to allow Sunday opening under Defence Regulation 42B. The Watch Committee quickly agreed terms with cinema managers: cinemas would pay 1s 6d per seat per year to charities; 5 per cent of these payments would be allocated to the Cinematograph Charity Fund and the remainder to charities determined by the Watch Committee.

The referendum was generally held to have been a fair fight. 'We feel,' said the Rev. O. L. F. Wade for the losers, 'like an amateur team which has run a crack professional team to a draw. But the committee does not feel it has been let down, although it was beaten.'[11]

The point of most general interest is that the public meeting was not the perfunctory prelude to the referendum envisaged by Samuel. Despite the obvious presence of more than a hundred objectors, a full debate was held and the votes were carefully counted. Nor would it have been easy to persuade those who attended to go home without a debate. Despite its excellent conduct, the Halifax meeting confirmed that the numbers had become too great. Rather more than 2,000 got into the Victoria Hall, while nearly as many again were left outside. Other towns did not have halls that would take as many as 2,000. Nor, in large urban communities, was it possible to be sure that all those present at a meeting, or even all those who spoke, were local-government electors. By joining the queue early, one side's supporters could pack a hall and produce an unrepresentative vote. And the Halifax meeting was held before the development of Rentamob. If public meetings had not now been abolished, the statutory hundred objectors might find themselves excluded.

LOCAL REFERENDA ON LOCAL INITIATIVE

The establishment of public libraries, the promotion of Private Bills, the closing and Sunday opening of pubs, the Sunday opening of cinemas— these are the only general subjects on which local referenda have been expressly provided for by statute. In addition, it remains open to a local authority to propose the holding of a referendum as a means of meeting any statutory obligation.

Under the Education Act 1944 (as amended by the Education Act 1968) local education authorities are required to submit proposals to the Secretary of State if they wish to change the character of a school. The last Labour Government was encouraging local authorities, through Department of Education and Science Circular 10/65,[12] to make secondary schools comprehensive. When the Conservatives were returned to power in 1970, the Department issued Circular 10/70[13] cancelling Circular 10/65 and declaring that 'Authorities will now be freer to determine the shape of secondary provision in their areas', and concluding: 'Full opportunities should be given to parents to make their views known before decisions are reached.'

Under the influence of Circular 10/70, several referenda were held in Buckinghamshire on whether comprehensive schooling should be introduced (with results in its favour). Education in Buckinghamshire was the responsibility of Divisional Executives whose areas were different from the local-government ones. The first referendum concerned the whole of the area administered by the Eton Divisional Executive— the areas of both the Eton Urban District and Eton Rural Councils. The second referendum was carried out by the Amersham and Chesham Divisional Executive in part of its area from which pupils attend a particular secondary school. Each referendum was conducted by the Divisional Executive Officer acting in accordance with the instructions of the Divisional Executive.

The expenses of holding a local referendum were incurred under Section 6 of the Local Government (Financial Provisions) Act 1963. This dealt with the power of local authorities to incur expenditure for certain purposes not otherwise authorized. The relevant provision was re-enacted virtually unchanged in Section 137 of the Local Government Act 1972, which took effect from 1 April 1974.

When, however, the question arose of a referendum on a swimming bath in 1966, the Urban District Councils Association took counsel's opinion:

> Under s.6 of the Local Government (Financial Provisions) Act, 1963, the local authority are to form an opinion as to whether expenditure for a purpose is in the interests of their area. They are not empowered to form an opinion to spend money on asking the electors to form an opinion, in my opinion.

This left the law on local referenda, if counsel was right, where it had been before the Local Government (Financial Provisions) Act 1963. And an earlier counsel's opinion, obtained by the Urban District Councils Association when an urban district council considered holding a referendum on its plan to petition for incorporation as a municipal borough, had declared:

> A council has no power to expend any money whatever on a referendum otherwise than in connection with a Parliamentary Bill or under the Sunday Entertainments Act, 1932, in my opinion. The purpose of electing councillors is that the council shall speak for the electorate. Therefore, even if the referendum were to be held simultaneously with the local elections, any money spent in connection with it would be spent unlawfully.

The Airdrie Town Council asked its electors in a postal referendum on 23 February 1939: 'Are you prepared to sell the gas undertaking to Coatbridge Gas Company or to any other firm or company?' The Council's judgement in holding the referendum was vindicated when no less than 48.4 per cent of the electors voted—2,648 No and 758 Yes. The referendum cost about £70, which appears to have been taken out of the gas account without incurring the disapproval of the auditors. Some local authorities, however, have indulged in manifestly illegal practices. I have it on good authority that a small burgh in Fife once held a referendum by adding a question about a public lavatory to the ballot-papers for the annual municipal elections.

Counsel's opinion on the 1963 and 1972 Acts is not binding in law. Some local authorities may not even know of its existence. As late as 1974, Teignmouth Town Council was proposing to hold a referendum under the 1972 Act on whether to build a breakwater out to sea at the mouth of the Teign. The idea was abandoned after local-government reorganization brought Teignmouth under the larger Teignbridge District Council. Penarth Town Council found a way when in 1959 it wanted to hold a referendum on whether Penarth should be merged with Cardiff. When it was advised that it had no authority to incur expense in connection with a referendum, the local Chamber of Trade conducted one for it on a voluntary basis. Five weeks after a well-attended public meeting in the Paget Rooms, unpaid helpers delivered voting forms to each household. The forms were collected a day or so later. A majority against merging with Cardiff—a majority of Hitlerian but genuine proportions—successfully influenced the Local Government Commission.

FUTURE OF LOCAL REFERENDA

However commendable the legal ingenuity and practical enterprise of some local authorities, the uncertainty of the law on local referenda is undesirable and unnecessary. Even Buckinghamshire's referenda on comprehensive schooling received no sanction from the central Government. The Department of Education and Science heard of them only informally. Whether or not they were legal presumably turns on whether sanction for a referendum was implied by: 'Full opportunities should be given to parents to make their views known before decisions are reached.' Soon the only indisputably legal local referenda may be those on the Sunday opening of Welsh pubs.

A major local-government reform was followed by low polls. We speak of the need to stimulate interest in local government while suppressing the obvious means. There is no reason to doubt electors would like to have an influence on major development schemes and the subsidy of public transport in the areas where they live. But they have more difficulty in voting on the issues that concern them in local elections than in a general election. Where local government is dominated by party politics, the choice before the electors is determined by

33

national issues. Where it is free of party politics, most electors are unlikely to discover the views of candidates on particular issues. They will be lucky if they get any information at all about local issues. Competition for votes in a referendum would be the best guarantee of their being given information. An Act should be passed not merely to allow but to encourage local authorities to hold referenda on their own initiative. The central Government should meet a proportion of the costs.

Such permissive legislation, while an advance, would not be enough. Regrettably most local authorities are not going to want to hold referenda when they should. The advocates of a referendum would need to win a local-government election in order to get a referendum. At best the opportunity of separating particular issues from party politics would be lost.[14] At worst, with one party permanently in control, there would be no hope of winning an election, and hence no hope of securing a referendum. It should be made possible for, say, a quarter of the councillors to demand a referendum. This would give a purpose in life simultaneously to local-government oppositions and electors. It would keep local authorities responsive to public opinion. Even where one party holds all the seats, it would have to reckon with rebellions by its own councillors on particular issues. If there is Scottish and Welsh devolution, a similar provision for demanding referenda could protect their Parliaments from acquiring the character of the old Stormont.

As a protection against apathy, the result of a local referendum should be treated as valid only if the winning side secured the votes of 15 per cent of the registered electors. Otherwise the local authority should be free to ignore the result. Of course local authorities are not sovereign states. There might be provision for a local authority having reason to disregard the result of a referendum to appeal to the central Government for a dispensation.

Generally speaking, referenda should not be allowed on the same subject without an interval of, say, two years. (Intervals laid down for the statutory local referenda varied from twelve months, under the Public Libraries Acts, to seven years, under the 1961 Licensing Act dealing with Welsh Sunday opening.) There should be an independent Referendum Commission by analogy with the Boundary Commission to oversee the conduct of local referenda (and veto referenda on manifestly trivial as well as illegal subjects). It would have to approve the phrasing of a referendum question and be satisfied that electors were being given relevant information and allowed to know the opposing arguments. The Referendum Commission should perform the same role in relation to national referenda. The proposals I have made for local referenda are in miniature those I shall make for national referenda in Chapter 12.

4
IRELAND

WHEN ENOCH POWELL suggested, in 1973, that Conservative Marketeers should vote Labour in a general election, he cited 1886. This was the year in which Gladstone's Home Rule Bill was defeated by 343 votes to 313, some 93 Liberals voting against it. Although the Bill provided for an Irish Parliament, most powers of taxation were reserved to Westminster; and Joseph Chamberlain, the dissenting Liberals' leader, himself favoured devolution for Ireland. None the less the split was permanent. The Conservatives and Liberal Unionists (Liberals who believed in the union of Ireland and Great Britain) became allies, as did the Gladstone Liberals and Parnellites. The Conservatives were in office for the next nineteen years—though their continuance in office for the ten years after 1895 is properly attributable to the Liberals' advocacy of local option in the temperance cause.

It was probably in August 1885 that Gladstone finally decided the Irish must have Home Rule. For a time he confided in few. The House of Lords could be expected to oppose it. Recalling how Conservative Governments had introduced Catholic Emancipation in 1829, repealed the Corn Laws in 1846, and passed the Second Reform Act in 1867, he plotted to keep a Conservative Government in power so that it might grant Home Rule. Once his plot failed, there could be little chance of Home Rule unless the powers of the Lords were first restricted. Queen Victoria would hardly be willing to create enough Liberal peers to provide a majority for Home Rule in the Lords. Yet Dicey, the leading constitutional lawyer of the time, was sufficiently fearful of Home Rule to suggest that it be put to a referendum of the entire United Kingdom.[1] And Gladstone, in the election of 1892, 'confidently calculated on a majority in the Commons large enough to overawe the House of Lords'.[2] The election produced a majority for Home Rule of only forty. Gladstone's second Home Rule Bill passed its third reading in September 1893 by only thirty-four votes. A week later the Lords, anything but overawed, rejected it by 417 votes to 41. Still not reassured, Dicey expressed concern that 'a majority of from 30 to 40 warranted the attempt to dissolve the Union between Great Britain and Ireland'[3] and again argued for a referendum.

With the passing of the Parliament Act 1911 the Lords could no longer veto a Home Rule Bill: they could only, by rejecting it in successive sessions, delay it for two years. The Irish MPs, on whom the Liberal Government depended for a majority, had become almost attached to Westminster. A third Home Rule Bill introduced in 1912 offered a federal solution—with the Irish having their own Parliament and sending forty-two MPs to Westminster as well. (The eventual status of Northern Ireland was modelled on this Bill.) Between 1886 and 1912, however, agitation among the Protestants in the Northern counties had developed a determination, at once loyalist and mutinous, to resist Home Rule by force, while on the Republican side the extra-parliamentary Sinn Fein had gained in strength. The first draft of the 1912 Bill nearly included provision for any or all of the Northern counties, subject to the result of plebiscites, to contract out of Home Rule. Redmond, now Leader of the Irish MPs, would not agree to it, whether because of his own devotion to a united Ireland or because of his fear of Sinn Fein. The Liberal Cabinet hoped that in the end he would decide that half (or rather more than half) a loaf was better than no bread. They should have remembered the Old Testament mother who would have given her baby away rather than have it cut in half.

While the passage of the Bill was delayed by the Lords, Sir Edward Carson and Andrew Bonar Law developed the opposition in the North. Dicey in 1913 backed a demand by Bonar Law and Lord Landsdowne that the King should force a dissolution by dismissing Asquith. It has to be admitted that Dicey had no judgement on Ireland, which lessens the authority of his advocacy of the referendum. In March 1914, when the Bill was presented to the Lords for the third time under the Parliament Act, Asquith revealed his intention to propose an amendment allowing each of the Northern counties to hold a plebiscite with a view to contracting out of Home Rule for six years.

> The theory of it was that before it expired the electors of the United Kingdom would have been twice consulted [not later than December 1915 and December 1920] and if they twice ratified Ulster's inclusion she would have no grievance. But in fact, of course, to make the inclusion of Ulster the sole issue at a general election in, say, 1919 would have been scarcely practicable, and if possible, most undesirable.[4]

At all events the Protestants demanded the right of the Northern counties to contract out of Home Rule without a time limit. The Amending Bill, introduced in June, led to further negotiations. The Protestants made some concessions. Instead of plebiscites in individual counties, there could be a single plebiscite for an area which was the present Northern Ireland minus South Armagh, South Fermanagh and perhaps South Down. It this area contracted out of Home Rule, it should be without a time limit; but there would be an option for it to unite with the rest of Ireland by plebiscite at any time. Redmond rejected the offer. The issue was still unresolved when the First World War broke out. The Home Rule Act was duly passed, but with a provision that it should not come into force until a year after the end of the war.

During the war the extremists gained yet greater strength. The Government of Ireland Act 1920 gave North and South separate Parliaments with Home Rule. There was civil war in the South over whether Partition should be accepted. The Anglo-Irish Treaty of 1921 gave Ireland Dominion status and Northern Ireland the right to opt out. Dominion status, unlike Home Rule, meant fiscal, military and naval autonomy—virtual Independence. The Irish Free State was brought into existence on 5 December 1922, and on 5 December the Northern Ireland Parliament exercised the right to opt out. No plebiscite had been held.

In view of its history, it is fitting that in Ireland there should have been held the first referendum in the United Kingdom on a more than local scale. On 8 March 1973, under the provisions of the Northern Ireland (Border Poll) Act 1972, 61 per cent of the electors, guarded by armed policemen and soldiers, went to the polls, where the ballot-papers required them to put a cross signifying assent to one or other of the following questions:

Do you want Northern Ireland to remain part of the United Kingdom?

Do you want Northern Ireland to be joined with the Republic of Ireland, outside the United Kingdom?

There were 591,820 votes for the *status quo* and 6,463 for a united Ireland (5,973 being spoiled). The huge majority for the *status quo* was attributable to Catholic abstentions. The British (Conservative) Government's purpose in holding the plebiscite was not to determine whether Northern Ireland should remain in the United Kingdom. At the time that was regarded as a foregone conclusion. It was to take the Border out of politics. During the fifty years of Northern Ireland's existence, the main issue between the parties had been Partition, and the Unionist Party had been permanently in power. The 1973 referendum was intended to be the first of a ten-yearly series. The hope was that, being able to vote for or against unification in periodical referenda, Northern Irish electors would vote Left or Right at elections, when the predominant parties would have members and supporters of both religions.

With all these arguments in favour of the Border referenda, the Commons had agreed to them only reluctantly. The most persuasive argument was that, since the Northern Ireland Parliament was suspended at the time proposed for the first one, the electors could not express their opinion without resort to unnatural practice. The precedent set in Northern Ireland prepared the Commons for the EEC referendum. If the referendum comes to be accepted as a permanent institution in the United Kingdom, some of the credit will belong to the Troubles.

At the time the first Border referendum was regarded as a failure. The Catholic abstentions were one reason. Another was that, in the subsequent elections for the new Northern Ireland Assembly, voting was largely sectarian. Before the year was out, however, the Unionist Party and the Social Democratic and Labour Party (the main Catholic party) formed a power-sharing Executive (which is to say a Coalition Government) with the new non-sectarian Alliance Party; and agreement was reached at Sunningdale with the Governments of the Republic and the United Kingdom on the formation of a Council of Ireland. The power-sharing Executive did not endure. Opposition in the North has prevented the formation of the Council of Ireland. Yet Northern Ireland politics will never be the same again. Co-operation between Protestants and Catholics and between Northern Ireland and the Republic has become politically possible.

Another secular change is that no British political party any longer wishes to retain Northern Ireland in the United Kingdom. British policy in Ireland used to be based on a mixture of imperialism and obligation to the Protestants. Only obligation is left, and this is not an enduring basis for a policy that requires the commitment of troops and the exposure of civilians to bombing. The Protestants in Northern Ireland know this and fear a sell-out. Their opposition to the Council of Ireland was aroused, not by the innocuous powers proposed for it, but by fear that it was the beginning of the imposition of Irish unification. Brian Faulkner's power-sharing Executive was brought down by opposition to the Council of Ireland combined with the ability to argue that it did not have majority support. The only realistic policy left to the British Government is to tell the truth and supplement it with judicious use of referenda. Let it declare:

The peace and prosperity of Ireland are indivisible. The *long-term* aim of the British Government is therefore the unification of Ireland.

But unification will never be allowed without the consent in a referendum of a majority of the electors in Northern Ireland. Indeed any and every change in the constitutional status of Northern Ireland must be subject to the consent of the electors in a referendum.

The British Government will co-operate with the Government

of the Republic of Ireland in creating conditions in which unification is acceptable to the majority in the North.

Even without such a declaration, the time is foreseeable when one of the planned ten-yearly referenda will produce a majority for unification. The Catholics constitute a third of the population of Northern Ireland. Within decades their higher birth rate may so far exceed their higher emigration rate as to give them a majority. It is likely too that increasing numbers of Protestants will favour unification, at least on a federal basis. Ireland suffers economically from Partition. Common membership of the EEC will emphasize the economic advantages of co-operation. It is a remarkable fact that the 5 per cent of Protestants living in the Republic have suffered virtually no persecution or discrimination. The Protestants in the North have nothing to fear from unification.

The first development in relations between Northern Ireland and the Republic should be modelled on the early Swiss leagues and the Swiss Confederation before 1798. There should be a Council of Ireland. Delegates to it from Northern Ireland and the Republic should be bound by instructions and take only unanimous decisions. Though this Council of Ireland would have literally no powers of its own, it should be introduced only after acceptance in a referendum in the North. When there had been some years' experience of such a Council of Ireland, it might be possible to give it discretion to take majority decisions in small matters, as the Council of Ministers of the EEC now does—but only again after the consent of the people of Northern Ireland had been obtained in a referendum.

Eventually Northern Ireland might leave the United Kingdom; a federal Government of Ireland might have responsibility for foreign affairs and defence, while the Governments of Northern Ireland and the Republic retained domestic powers. Who knows but that a united Ireland and Great Britain might then freely form a federal council in which at first the delegates were bound by instructions and took only unanimous decisions?

There would be protests from Protestant militants when the British Government declared itself in favour of long-term unification. But since they suppose it to be already, and since what they fear is imposed unification, a credible promise that unification would never be imposed on them would be reassuring. They would have little cause for complaint. Protestant belief has always been in the righteousness of the majority, and this would be respected.

The Provisional IRA's constitutional demands (as distinct from its demands about internment and the withdrawal of British troops) have been moderate and realistic. The promise of progress towards federal Government and the detachment of Northern Ireland from the United

Kingdom would probably induce the IRA to abandon violence permanently. This would make it possible to end internment and withdraw British troops. Certainly the commitment of the British Government to long-term unification would satisfy the aspirations of most of the people in the Irish Republic. If the IRA did not abandon violence, it would find itself without the tacit support that in the past has been its ultimate strength.

One difficulty must be anticipated. Before the first of the planned series of referenda on the Border, Edward Heath said:

> These plebiscites will be in addition to, and not in substitution for, the provisions in the Ireland Act, 1949, which require the consent of the Northern Ireland Parliament to any change in the Border. This position is not prejudiced by the temporary prorogation of that Parliament.[5]

This guarantee was subsequently incorporated in the Northern Ireland (Temporary Provisions) Act 1972. Even an Assembly elected by proportional representation might have a majority against unification when a majority of the electors were in favour. Apart from the moral objections to ignoring the result of a referendum, the Unionists could not have been confident the British Government would do it. This difficulty was removed by the Northern Ireland Constitution Act 1973, which repealed the relevant provision in the 1949 Act and also repealed the 1972 Act. Northern Ireland can now cease to be part of the United Kingdom without the consent of its Parliament but not, under the 1973 Act, without the consent of the majority of the electors of Northern Ireland voting in a referendum. The outstanding difficulty concerns the referenda. William Whitelaw said of them:

> The simple point must be made that the change could not be made without the consent of the majority of the people voting in the poll. But if consent was given by a very narrow majority it would clearly be a matter for the House, and no doubt for the Republic. That would be bound to be so. It would not automatically happen. It does not automatically happen. It cannot automatically happen. It would have to be a matter for this House to decide the constitutional change. The poll of itself would not do it.

It is arguable that Northern Ireland should be united with the Republic only with the support of 55 per cent of the electors—or perhaps only with the support of simple majorities in successive referenda with a minimum of a year between them. But the time to argue it, and to legislate for it, is now, not when the result of the referendum has been announced. Civil wars have been caused in Ireland by less scope for misunderstanding than that.

40

5
NATIONAL REFERENDA
THAT MIGHT HAVE BEEN

INTERREGNUM

BRITISH CONSTITUTIONAL HISTORY shows continuity except for a small aberration in the seventeenth century. Though the King was replaced by a Protector and the Lords temporarily abolished, the manner of government and the relation between Head of State and Parliament remained much as under the Tudors and preceding Stuarts—except that Cromwell, with a better army, could be even more dictatorial. Of more interest to us is what nearly happened—what might have happened if John Hampden had survived the wounds he sustained on Chalgrove Field to exert his influence against Cromwell's and prevent a purge of those in the army who disagreed with the generals. Puritanism gave rise simultaneously to the concepts of rule by God's elect and of a democracy in which power was delegated upwards. We have seen how the New England town meeting developed from the church covenants of the early settlers. In England in 1647, not long after the first emigrants had departed for New England, the Agitators, who were the representatives of the rank and file in Cromwell's army and allies of the Levellers, presented to the Council of the Army the Agreement of the People.

The Agreement of the People asserted the rights, not only of Parliament, but of the electors. Parliament's power was 'inferior only to theirs who chose them'.[1] There were to be biennial (single-chamber) Parliaments—which is to say that a Parliament could not extend its own lifetime. Parliament should not be empowered to interfere with certain fundamental rights, which included religious toleration, freedom from conscription, and the prohibition of privilege (in that all men were to be equally subject to the law). These fundamental rights were in effect a written Constitution. There was no provision for amending it, nor indeed for dealing with attempted breaches of it. The assumption was that, if Parliament sought to abuse its power, the people would disobey it. MPs were seen as delegates. The drafters of the Agreement of the People realized that the King had restrained Parliament no less than Parliament the King. Without the King, Parliament could become tyrannical. It may be said that the Agreement of the People switched from English to Swiss, or from Norman to Saxon, democracy; and

41

that it anticipated the Americans by more than a hundred years in substituting a written Constitution for the King's (or Governor's) veto.

A more elaborate version of the Agreement of the People in 1649 provided for a substantial quorum in Parliament and for male household suffrage (roughly equivalent to the franchises introduced by the Reform Acts of 1867 and 1884). Moreover, it anticipated the Americans further by providing for a referendum on itself. Commissioners were

> to take care for the orderly taking of all voluntary subscriptions to this Agreement, by fit persons to be employed for that purpose in every parish; who are to return the subscription so taken to the persons that employed them, keeping a transcript thereof to themselves; and those persons, keeping like transcripts, to return the original subscriptions to the respective Commissioners . . .[2]

Even today we 'subscribe' to opinions. The subscriptions envisaged in the Agreement of the People would have had the appearance of petitions. The two reasons we should regard them as referenda instead of petitions are that state officials, not private individuals, were to collect signatures, and that they were to approach all the electors. A petition is part of a continuing process of persuasion and, unlike a referendum, implies no respect for majority decision.

To the best of my knowledge nothing in the nature of a referendum had been proposed in Britain before the Agreement of the People. The Scottish Covenants were more than petitions, in that signing them involved a solemn commitment to a cause. Opposing Charles I's imposition on the Church of Scotland of episcopacy and practices alien to Presbyterianism, the Covenanters were rebels within Great Britain but represented official Scotland. On the other hand, the Covenants were propaganda. Their noble and ecclesiastical signatories would have been the last to think of deferring to majority decision.

LORDS' POWERS

By the twentieth century the Lords had much less power than the Commons. Convention allowed it no right to interfere with a Money Bill and its right to veto other Bills was problematical. Gladstone had wanted to make a 'Peers *versus* People' issue of Home Rule. His 'faint-hearted colleagues' restrained him but 'had nothing better to suggest than to continue "filling up the cup" of Lords' iniquitous vetoes on their bills in the forlorn hope that the peers would eventually overplay their hand and provoke public resentment'.[3] The hope was no longer forlorn once Lloyd George became Chancellor of the Exchequer. By taunting the House of Lords, he induced it to reject his People's Budget of 1909, a clear breach of convention. The Liberals held an election on the Lords' powers in January 1910. They lost the overall majority they had won in 1906, but had 275 seats to the Conservatives' (or Unionists') 273, while Labour had 40 and the Irish Nationalists 82.

The Liberals could rely on both Labour and the Nationalists for support—the Nationalists because the Lords stood between them and Home Rule. The new Government introduced the Parliament Bill to deny the Lords any power over Money Bills and allow them only to reject ordinary Bills in two successive sessions. The Lords would only be able to delay ordinary Bills for two years, not veto them— and by this time the Sovereign was a Constitutional Monarch, not given to vetoing Bills either.

When a veto over Legislation disappears, the need is felt to replace it by some other restraint. The interregnum afforded one example, the Independence of the American Colonies another. At a conference held in 1910 to try to resolve the constitutional crisis the Conservatives proposed that organic Bills—constitutional amendments, so to speak—should, if twice rejected by the Lords, be put to referendum. They were influenced by Dicey, who earlier advocated a referendum on Home Rule:

> They [the Conservatives] did not suspect the Government of wishing to abolish the Crown, or to change the Protestant Succession, or even, once its passage was secured, to amend the Parliament Bill. What they were interested in was Home Rule. This was a practical issue, and their dominant interest at the conference was to prevent the easing of its passage.[4]

The Liberals themselves prepared legislation for a referendum on the Parliament Bill. The Lords, to prevent its powers being reduced, would obviously reject the Parliament Bill. The evidence of a referendum might help persuade the King to agree to create enough Liberal peers to get the Bill through the Lords. In the event George V, who had to deal with the crisis immediately on succeeding to the throne, asked that a second general election be held on the issue. During the campaign the Conservatives persisted with their advocacy of the referendum. Opposing the referendum spoiled the Liberals' image as the purer democrats and exposed them to the mockery of Arthur Balfour, the Conservative Leader. Challenged by Asquith, the Liberal Prime Minister, Balfour agreed to hold a referendum on tariff reform—and proposed that in return the Liberals should hold one on Home Rule.

Except as a means of preventing Home Rule, the Conservatives had little enthusiasm for the referendum. F. E. Smith (later Lord Birkenhead) said privately that it could only harm the Tory Party in the long run. Austen Chamberlain, who was unwell during the election campaign, complained of referendum sickness. Two years later Andrew Bonar Law, Balfour's successor as Conservative Leader, was to repudiate the referendum pledge on the ground that to negotiate food duties at a Colonial Conference and then submit them to a referendum would be unfair to the Colonies.[5]

The election, in December 1910, produced almost exactly the same result as the one in the previous January, and the Parliament Bill was re-introduced. The most active advocate of the referendum in the late nineteenth and early twentieth centuries was John St Loe Strachey, editor of *The Spectator*. He now engaged Edward Henry Pember, a constitutional lawyer, to draw up a Bill providing for the referendum. This was introduced in the Lords, as the Reference to the People Bill, on 2 March 1911 (the same day as the Parliament Bill had its second reading in the Commons) by Lord Balfour of Burleigh, chosen because he had a reputation for being shrewd and practical. His Bill provided that any Bill rejected by the Lords could be put to referendum by either the Lords or the Commons. It further provided that a Bill passed by both Houses could be put to referendum by not less than 200 MPs. This would have created an anomaly in that a Bill passed by the Lords could be put to referendum by a mere 200 MPs, while one rejected by the Lords could be put to referendum only by a majority in the Commons. Though seriously debated, the Reference to the People Bill was not proceeded with. It went too far for the Conservative leaders.

Less than six weeks later, in May, the official Opposition in the Commons put forward a new clause on the report stage of the Parliament Bill providing for referenda only on 'organic' Bills—such as affected the Crown, the Protestant Succession, the franchise, the distribution of seats or the powers of the two Houses of Parliament, or, indeed, which granted Home Rule to any of the constituent parts of the United Kingdom. The Government's majority enabled it to reject such amendments in the Commons. The House did, however, divide on the clause, those voting for it including Balfour, Bonar Law, Stanley Baldwin and Max Aitken (later Lord Beaverbrook).

Amendments to the Parliament Bill were taken in the Lords in June. Lord Lansdowne's amendment to introduce the referendum for 'organic' Bills was carried by 253 to 40. Lord Willoughby de Broke, moved and carried to a division an amendment providing for a general election as well as a referendum, but this also was too much for the Conservative leaders. As it was, the Lords had changed the Bill out of recognition. George v agreed that if necessary he would create more Liberal peers. Only then did the Conservatives capitulate and allow the Parliament Bill through the Lords.

EMPIRE FREE TRADE

Although Balfour was effectively tricked, in 1910, into agreeing to a referendum on tariff reform, the idea appealed to him on merit. Conservative MPs were divided on the issue. A referendum would resolve it and prevent dissension within the party. Twenty years later Baldwin was to reason in the same way.

In 1930 the policy of Empire Free Trade, backed by Lords Beaverbrook and Rothermere, which is to say by the *Daily Express* and *Daily Mail*, found much support within the Conservative Party. Empire Free Trade meant no tariffs within the Empire but tariffs against countries outside the Empire—in other words, an Empire Common Market. That the reluctance of the Dominions to lower tariffs against British goods made Empire Free Trade impracticable was little solace to Baldwin, on the defensive after losing the 1929 election. He himself favoured the extension of imperial trade but would not commit himself to putting taxes on foreign food, which could both split the Conservative Party and lose it electoral support.

Churchill wanted Baldwin to hold four by-elections on the issue, two in the North, one in an agricultural constituency, and one near London—a miniature general election. J. C. C. (later Lord) Davidson, chairman of the Conservative Party, warned him that this would split the party irrevocably. At a private meeting held on 3 March 1930 Beaverbrook told Baldwin that if he would agree to a referendum his problem would be solved. Davidson (who was under attack himself and was later forced to resign) had little sympathy with referenda but encouraged the plan on tactical grounds. In February Beaverbrook and Rothermere had published the manifesto of the United Empire Party. Beaverbrook planned to contest fifty seats at the next general election. Baldwin felt he must prevent this. As an alternative to a referendum he suggested two general elections with a Dominions Conference in between; but the agreement reached was that the Conservative Party should support Empire Free Trade subject to a referendum on food taxes and that Beaverbrook should abandon his new party. The next day, in a major speech at the Hotel Cecil, Baldwin declared:

A General Election is a party fight, and a treaty would become part of a party programme.

If such a matter were treated as a shuttlecock in party politics, it might damage Imperial relations, perhaps for generations.

For some time past I have been trying to discover if it is not possible for these big questions concerning our Imperial relationship to be taken out of the arena of party politics.

I believe there is only one way out, the referendum.

A referendum ought not to involve the fate of the Government.

The people can give their decision on its merits, for they know it does not involve a General Election.[6]

Five weeks later Davidson issued from Conservative Central Office a circular entitled *This is Baldwin's pledge to you*. Baldwin, like the present Labour Government, intended the result of his referendum to be binding:

There will be no food taxes at the General Election and no food taxes ever without a direct vote of the people.

What Baldwin asks is that you should give him power to go into conference with the Dominions in order to make a bargain which will enable us to sell more manufactured goods to them, and so create more employment and more wages for our workers.

If, in return for those benefits to our workers, the Dominions say to us that they can supply us with food and raw materials that we need, and ask us to help them by putting taxes on foreign foodstuffs and allowing theirs in free—then Baldwin will put that bargain before the electors of the country by means of a referendum.

That means that every voter will be asked to fill in a ballot card saying either 'Yes' or 'No' to the proposed bargain and the votes of the people will decide the question . . .[7]

Beaverbrook did not feel this committed the Conservative Party sufficiently to Empire Free Trade. Like the contemporary anti-Marketeers, he had seen the referendum as a weapon against his opponents, whereas Baldwin had seen it as a peace treaty. In a speech at Hastings in May, Beaverbrook asked that the plan for a referendum be abandoned: 'The Central Office apears to me to be using the referendum, not as a spear with which to fight for Empire Free Trade but as a shield behind which to shelter itself.'[8] Baldwin kept to his policy until October. Then at the Imperial Conference the Canadian Prime Minister, Richard (later Lord) Bennett, proposed a 10 per cent preferential increase in all duties, present or future, levied on goods from outside the Empire. Baldwin saw political advantage in declaring: 'Whatever the Socialist Government may do, the Conservative Party accepts the principle put forward with such weight and unanimity.'[9] The pledge on the referendum was tacitly though never formally withdrawn.

PROLONGING THE COALITION
The Parliament Act 1911 has left the Lords with a veto only over Bills to prolong the lifetime of Parliament. This is necessary to prevent a tyrannical House of Commons from voting itself in power for ever. Unlike a written Constitution laying down an absolute limit to the lifetime of a Parliament, the Lords' veto is flexible. In an emergency the Lords can allow the Commons to exceed the five-year limit. It did so during both World Wars. By 1945 Parliament had been sitting for ten years. After the defeat of Germany in May, Labour indicated that it did not want to maintain the Coalition Government beyond the autumn. Churchill wrote to Attlee asking him to maintain it until the defeat of Japan and suggesting that a referendum might be held on whether the lifetime of Parliament should be further extended.

As a Liberal in 1910-11 Churchill had opposed the substitution of the referendum for the Lords' veto on constitutional matters. Now he was proposing that a referendum should be held on the one aspect of the Constitution on which the Lords' veto had been preserved. He had never, however, been an implacable opponent of the referendum. We have seen that the Liberal Government of which he was a member considered holding a referendum on the Parliament Bill itself. At that time he himself proposed a referendum among women on votes for women. Later, as a Conservative, he was an enthusiastic supporter of Baldwin's proposal to hold a referendum on food taxes arising from Empire Free Trade.

Attlee replied (in part):

> I do not think that it would be right or possible to obtain from Parliament another prolongation of its life. I could not consent to the introduction into our national life of a device so alien to all our traditions as the referendum, which has only too often been the instrument of Nazism and Fascism. Hitler's practices in the field of referenda and plebiscites can hardly have endeared these expedients to the British heart.[10]

While Attlee could be expected to reject Churchill's proposal as inexpedient, his vehemence manifested a genuine Labour antipathy to the referendum. In their *Industrial Democracy*,[11] published in 1897, the Webbs recalled how the early trade unions suffered from the referendum (on administrative or judicial decisions about benefit claims as well as on legislative rules) and from the initiative. Clifford Sharp, in his Fabian Tract, *The Case against the Referendum*,[12] published in 1911, argued that the referendum would lead to the initiative—which the experience of other countries has not confirmed.

Essentially Labour's opposition to the referendum was a reaction to the Conservatives' advocacy of it in 1910-11. In the use they proposed for the referendum, the Conservatives were avowedly seeking to prevent radical or socialist legislation. Labour therefore opposed the referendum as conservative at the time when Left-wing parties on the continent and in America were adding it to their programmes as a means of passing radical legislation. It was also a time when Labour was associated with guild-socialist, or participatory, ideas. It made Labour Party members vulnerable in argument, as are Liberals today when asked to reconcile opposition to the referendum with advocacy of community politics. Baldwin's willingness to hold a referendum in 1930 appeared to confirm the Labour syllogism: what the Conservatives want is bad; the Conservatives want the referendum; therefore the referendum is bad. Labour's prejudice was both to influence and be influenced by the EEC debate.

6
MARKET MEMBERSHIP

WHEN HAROLD MACMILLAN announced in August 1961 that he wanted Britain to join the EEC, it was a Conservative MP, Anthony Fell, who called him a national disaster. Right-wing Conservatives objected to joining because it meant sacrificing sovereignty as such. Left-wing Labour MPs objected to sacrificing sovereignty to an organization with restrictions on subsidies and with predominantly Right-wing Governments. Both Conservative and Labour opponents of the EEC objected to diminishing the Commonwealth. The Conservative but not the Labour opponents included tentative advocates of a referendum. At the end of a two-day debate only five MPs—and only one Conservative, Anthony Fell—voted against the Government's motion. About twenty Conservative MPs abstained. Rather fewer Labour MPs refrained from voting for an Opposition amendment emphasizing obligations to the Commonwealth and the European Free Trade Association (EFTA).

The European Economic Community had been established in March 1957 by France, West Germany, Italy, Belgium, the Netherlands and Luxembourg. In August 1961 the Irish Republic applied for membership, while Britain and Denmark more circumspectly asked for negotiations about membership. In April 1962 Norway also asked for negotiations about membership.

The British negotiations, begun in October 1961, were conducted by Edward Heath, Lord Privy Seal in Macmillan's Cabinet. In January 1963, when the negotiations were proving successful, de Gaulle effectively vetoed British membership on the ground that Britain was an island. Brussels diplomats comforted themselves with the story of the bridegroom who, having insisted on inspecting his bride in the nude, called off the marriage because she had blue eyes.

Harold Wilson was always more disposed to join the EEC in office than in Opposition. After preliminary talks with EEC leaders, Wilson asked the Commons in May 1967 to support an application for membership. Labour had no mandate for this move: joining the EEC had not been in its manifesto at the 1966 election. With Edward Heath leading the Opposition, however, the Commons complied by 488 votes to 62.

Britain, the Irish Republic, Norway and Denmark all made formal application to join the EEC in May 1967. The other three countries were all to hold referenda on joining. In Britain, despite the fact that the Government had no mandate for its application, there was no serious thought of a referendum.

The traditional Labour antipathy to referenda persisted. When a Conservative MP, Harold Gurden, moved for leave to bring in a Bill 'to provide for a referendum to be held with a general election'[1] (he had in mind, not the EEC, but the traditional free-vote issues), Denis Coe, a Labour backbencher argued that referenda 'would be or could be used by the Government of the day to appeal over the heads of the Chamber, just as in ancient Greece the Charismic leadership of the day appealed to the mob and tried to get Greece away from the idea of a representative Chamber'.[2]

Britain's application for membership of the EEC looked academic when in November 1967 de Gaulle refused to negotiate about it. But in April 1969 de Gaulle resigned. In July, Georges Pompidou, the newly elected French President, said he did not in principle oppose British entry.

As British interest in joining intensified, more was heard of a possible referendum, though without encouragement in high places. Harold Wilson told Neil Marten, Conservative, that a referendum was 'contrary to our traditions in this country'.[3] He told Raphael Tuck, Labour:

Hon. Members on either side of the House do not usually feel that referenda are a way in which to conduct our public affairs. I am sure that a referendum would give 100 per cent. support for increasing expenditure on every item. It would give 100 per cent. support for abolishing income tax.[4]

Another Conservative MP, Bruce Campbell, moved for leave to bring a Bill 'to allow the electors of Great Britain and Northern Ireland the right to decide by way of referendum whether Great Britain should join the European Economic Community'.[5] His argument was impeccable even if his forecast was dubious:

The three major political parties have all declared themselves to be in favour of this country joining the Common Market. It therefore follows that this question will never be an election issue and the people will have absolutely no chance of ever being able to express their views on it through the ballot box at a General Election.[6]

Bruce Campbell's argument had the greater force because the opinion polls showed ever-increasing public opposition to joining—with, ironically, more support among Labour voters. The motion was lost by 160 votes to 55. The fifty-five supporters of a referendum included Jo Grimond, former Leader of the Liberal Party; Douglas Jay, who had resigned from the Labour Government over the EEC; Sir Derek Walker-Smith, a Conservative Privy Councillor; and Philip Goodhart, Conservative author of an earlier book on the referendum.[7]

By the beginning of 1970 both Government and Opposition Marketeers were embarrassed by the polls' evidence of increasing opposition to joining the EEC. In a debate on an EEC White Paper, Reginald Maudling, the Conservative Deputy Leader, expressed reservations about opinion polls, but continued:

> Nevertheless, there is no doubt that there has been a strong and definite move of public opinion against the Common Market ... We in this House, if it is to be a democracy, cannot disregard the views of our constituents and of the public at large.[8]

Edward Heath told the British Chamber of Commerce in Paris on 5 May 1970: 'Nor would it be in the interest of the Community that its enlargement should take place except with the full-hearted consent of the Parliaments and peoples of the new member countries.' Speaking shortly afterwards on a television Election Forum he said: 'No British Government could possibly take this country into the Common Market against the wish of the British people.'[9]

Because of the unanimity of the official party policies, the EEC was not a campaign issue in 1970. Nor, for the same reason, was a referendum. The election, held in June, was unexpectedly won by the Conservatives. Edward Heath, the bride left at the altar in 1963, was free to marry into the European family after all, but had undertaken not to do so without parental consent.

Negotiations between the prospective entrants—Britain, the Irish Republic, Denmark and Norway—began on 30 June. Responsibility for EEC negotiations was held from the end of July by Geoffrey Rippon, as Chancellor of the Duchy of Lancaster. It was held briefly before that by Anthony Barber, until he became Chancellor of the Exchequer on the sudden death of Iain Macleod.

It might have been expected that advocacy of a referendum by anti-EEC Conservatives, including some of the extreme Right, would exacerbate Labour's fear of demagoguery. But it was difficult to maintain such fears when numerous other countries were holding referenda without coming to harm. De Gaulle had resigned after a manifest failure to make demagogic use of a referendum. It would have been impolitic to imply that the British people were more gullible or hysterical than the French.

Tony Benn, even while in office, developed the theme that Labour was the party of participation—the party that had faith in the judgement and responsibility of ordinary people. In May 1968 he made a major speech in which, like Harold Gurden, he advocated referenda on Bills traditionally submitted to a free vote. He was soon suggesting a referendum on the EEC, with the implication that it was a means of gaining support for membership. After Labour lost the 1970 election, its anti-EEC faction seized the initiative and Tony Benn joined it, still advocating a referendum. During this early period of the Heath Government both its Labour and Conservative advocates seem to have decided that a referendum should be consultative: in other words, the Government should not be bound by its result. Whether or not because its advocacy had been associated with Right-wing Conservatives, it took Tony Benn a surprisingly long time to gain support for a referendum among Labour anti-Marketeers. The European Communities (Referendum) Bill he presented in May 1971 made no progress in the Commons. The British way, it was assumed, was a free vote.

It was therefore surprising when Heath, as Prime Minister, implied that the Conservative Whips would be on for the EEC vote. Predictably Labour reacted by assuming it must put its own Whips on in opposition to joining. A pamphlet published by the Conservative Research Department in August 1971 explained why there would be no free vote:

A 'free vote' is normally reserved for matters which do not form an integral part of the Government's strategy so that the policy of the Government as a whole is not greatly affected. This is obviously not the case on this issue.[10]

Having explained that MPs should not be allowed to exercise their own judgement, the pamphlet proceeded immediately to dismiss the proposal for a referendum on the ground that 'It would be derogatory to the authority of Parliament, whose members have been elected to exercise their judgment on just such matters.'[11]

The essential EEC negotiations were completed within a year, on 23 June 1971. Britain was expected to join on 1 January 1973. At the end of July the Commons spent four days debating a White Paper recommending entry but took no vote. The Government was allowing three months for a great debate in the country.

The Labour Party presented a background paper, *The United Kingdom and the European Communities*, to its Annual Conference in October 1971. This made a concession to the arguments for a referendum. The crucial word is 'immediate':

If our Annual Conference opposes the terms, and the great parties are divided on the issue, we demand that the matter be subject to the will of the electorate through an immediate General Election.

Harold Wilson was now leading the Labour anti-Marketeers, on the ground that the terms negotiated by Geoffrey Rippon were unsatisfactory. Few were convinced of his sincerity. The charitable view was that he was acting to hold the Labour Party together. Those who

51

believed Wilson would have accepted the terms if he himself had been Prime Minister included Roy Jenkins, his former Chancellor of the Exchequer, Michael Stewart, his former Foreign Secretary, and George Thompson, who had actually been in charge of Labour's preliminary EEC negotiations. The Labour Conference voted five to one against entry on the terms negotiated.

Edward Heath was pleasantly surprised when the Conservative Conference voted eight to one in favour of entry. He decided to give Conservative MPs a free vote on entry after all. Labour was by now psychologically committed to opposition. There had been majorities against joining on the terms negotiated, not only at the Labour Conference, but in the Parliamentary Labour Party and the National Executive, not to mention the TUC. In the critical vote on 28 October, while Conservative MPs had a free vote, Labour MPs received a three-line whip. No less than sixty-nine Labour MPs defied the whip and voted for entry, while another twenty abstained. Five Liberals voted for entry and one against. Although thirty-nine Conservatives voted against entry and two abstained, the Government had a majority of 112 (356 votes to 244). The Lords approved the same motion by a majority of 393.

Roy Jenkins and other Labour Marketeers were bitterly reproached for voting according to their convictions. Moral considerations apart, it is uncertain that the Government would have been brought down even if Liberal and Labour Marketeers had voted against their beliefs and Conservative anti-Marketeers had none the less voted for theirs. A Government resigns if defeated on a vote of confidence. A vote on a major issue is usually equated with a vote of confidence, but joining the EEC was a special case, the more so since Conservative MPs were allowed a free vote. If defeated, the Government might have felt entitled to ask for a vote of confidence, which, with the support of its own anti-Marketeers, it would have won.

If Heath had made it clear from the outset that he would allow a free vote, Wilson would probably have assumed he should do the same. Heath would then have secured a larger majority for joining the EEC. There would still have been the problem that the Commons did not represent public opinion. But the two main parties would have been spared some internal dissension and the Commons some degradation.

Heath's original reluctance to allow a free vote appears to have been due solely to his proclivity for confrontation. Had it been Machiavellian, it would have been brilliant, for it split the Labour Party more severely than the Conservative. In 1970 Roy Jenkins had beaten Michael Foot for the Deputy Leadership by 133 votes to 67. After the EEC vote he retained it, but by only 140 to 126.

Having given notice that they would fight for their corner, the

Labour Marketeers then stayed in it. They decided that, having voted for EEC membership in principle, they were free to oppose the Government or abstain in votes on the actual European Communities Bill introduced in January 1972 after Britain, Denmark, the Irish Republic and Norway had all signed the Treaty of Accession. This was as difficult to defend as the inconsistency of former Labour Marketeers who had become anti-Marketeers. It put the European Communities Bill in jeopardy. The Government's majority on the second reading on 17 February 1972 fell to eight. This was the day a Labour MP assaulted Jeremy Thorpe, who was held to have wasted an opportunity to bring down the Tory Government they all opposed.

In April the Labour Shadow Cabinet decided to support the Conservative anti-Marketeers' demand for a referendum. By definition this would solve the problem that the Commons was unrepresentative of public opinion. It might also have been expected to resolve the Labour Party's own problems: if the issue was not going to be decided either at party meetings or in the Commons, party unity was no longer important. This was the principle on which Baldwin had proposed a referendum on Empire Free Trade.

But Wilson was not concerned, like Baldwin, to respect the integrity and retain the goodwill of both factions in his party. For the time being he had thrown in his lot with the anti-Marketeers, who interpreted the decision to demand a referendum as a further triumph. There was no suggestion that they would no longer coerce the Marketeers to vote with them in the Commons.

Roy Jenkins now resigned as Deputy Leader and as a member of the Shadow Cabinet. He felt the Labour Party was opposing entry to the EEC on principle, as distinct from criticizing the terms. Unlike Shirley Williams and some other Labour Marketeers, he was also opposed to a referendum as such. George Thompson and Harold Lever also resigned from the Shadow Cabinet. A number of other Labour Front Benchers resigned their roles as party spokesmen. One of them, Dick Taverne, was later to resign his seat as MP for Lincoln and regain it in the by-election as Democratic Labour candidate standing against the official Labour candidate.

In May 1972, shortly after the Labour resignations, the Irish Republic held a referendum in which the electors voted to join the EEC by 83 to 17 per cent, or nearly five to one, with a turnout of 71 per cent. The Irish referendum was obligatory under the Constitution and binding on the Government.

Norwegian accession to the EEC required, as a constitutional amendment, the support of three-quarters of MPs voting. There are no circumstances in which the Norwegian Constitution requires a referendum. Norway did, however, have precedents for referenda on important matters and held one on the EEC in September 1972. The electors voted by 53.5 to 46.5 per cent not to join the EEC, with a turnout of 77.7 per cent. Though this referendum was consultative only, the *Storting* (Parliament) had agreed in advance that it would respect the people's wishes and confirmed the decision. (Norway remains outside the EEC, and, partly thanks to North Sea Oil, appears to be thriving.) Since Trygve Bratteli, the Labour Prime Minister, had indicated he would treat the referendum as a vote of confidence, his Government resigned.

In October Denmark held a referendum. The Danish *Folketing* had already voted 141 to 37 in favour of membership. A referendum was necessary because less than five-sixths of MPs voted in favour (though Government and Opposition had agreed that a referendum should be held anyway). Membership of the EEC would have been rejected if opposed by a majority of those voting in the referendum and by not less than 30 per cent of the total electorate. In the event the Danes defied the Norwegian example and voted for membership by 63.3 to 36.7 per cent, with a turnout of nearly 90 per cent.

In the same week as the Danes held their referendum, the Labour Conference at Blackpool voted by nearly two to one that a future Labour Government should seek to renegotiate Britain's terms of entry and, whether or not successful, should let the British people vote on membership on the final terms in either a general election or a consultative referendum.

Without the decision to hold a referendum, this Conference would undoubtedly have decided that the next Labour Government should withdraw Britain from the EEC. Although the referendum had caused a split in the Shadow Cabinet in April, it prevented a bigger one in the whole party (including the Shadow Cabinet) six months later.

The European Communities Bill received the Royal Assent on 17 October. The United Kingdom actually joined the EEC, as well as Euratom and the European Coal and Steel Community, on 1 January 1973. On the eve of joining, the latest opinion poll, Opinion Research Centre for the BBC, showed 38 per cent in favour, 39 per cent opposed, and 23 per cent undecided. Opposition had evidently diminished, but it could not be contended that membership had the full-hearted consent of the British people. Though George Thompson agreed to become an EEC commissioner, the Labour Party as such decided to boycott the European Parliament at Strasbourg and declined to nominate the fifteen members it was entitled to send.

There was no feeling that Britain's entry to the EEC was irrevocable. The Labour Opposition did not accept membership, and it was only a question of time before there would be another Labour Government. The other members of the EEC would have had no great complaint if Britain had subsequently withdrawn. They would at no point have been deceived.

Britain's entry was contingent and, paradoxically, became a serious electoral issue only after the event. At Stockport on 8 June 1973 Enoch Powell, in a dramatic, brilliantly argued yet cryptic speech, implied that Conservatives opposed to the EEC should be willing to vote Labour at the next election if there was no anti-EEC Conservative candidate in their constituency. At the 1970 election, he recalled, the parties had contrived that the EEC should not be an issue:

> It would be quite otherwise if in 1973 or 1974 or 1975, the two main parties offered the electorate a choice. Nothing could then prevent the general election from being treated, by those electors who wished to do so, as a referendum; and there is plenty of reason to think that a large number of electors would wish to do so, and consider that they have already been denied what was their right....
>
> In the next Parliament will be completed the absorption of Britain into the new European State as one province along with others. Between there lies one event, one hurdle to be cleared, one barrier across the way—a general election. There is just the little matter of securing for all this, before it is irrecoverable and irreversible, what used to be considered as manifestly indispensable— the full-hearted consent of the British people. Or is that all over and done with, too? ... I would not conceal, even if I could, where my own counsel lies.... It is for us, and us alone, to determine if we will continue to be a free, self-governing people. I refuse to imagine that we shall answer no.[12]

Early in his speech Powell recalled the split in the Liberal Party in 1886, when Joseph Chamberlain and his followers opposed Home Rule and thereby introduced twenty years of Conservative Government. British politicians had been wont to quote 1886 as a warning of the consequences of party disloyalty. Powell unashamedly cited it as a precedent.

The implication of the Stockport speech was that anti-EEC Conservatives should vote Labour because Labour was anti-EEC. In his later speeches the emphasis shifted: anti-EEC Conservatives should vote Labour because Labour would offer the people a free choice either in a referendum or in a general election devoted to EEC membership.

The increasing talk about a referendum embarrassed the Liberals. They had always upheld the rights of the individual and in recent years had advocated community politics. It was to be expected they would favour a referendum. Jo Grimond did, but not Jeremy Thorpe, who had succeeded him as Liberal Leader. Answering a question from a viewer on a *Midweek* 'Phone-In' on 31 July 1973, Thorpe declared himself totally opposed to a referendum and implied that an election could be called after new terms of EEC membership had been negotiated But he warned that, if we had an election, then all the other issues such as the current cost of living and the balance of payments would get mixed up in it—which must have struck many viewers as a good reason for holding a referendum.

The Labour Conference in October 1973 was called on by Southampton Test to declare its opposition in principle to the EEC. The motion was defeated by only 3,316,000 to 2,800,000 votes. By a majority of five to one the Conference reaffirmed that there should be either an election or a referendum on the EEC and that meanwhile Labour should boycott its institutions. The two factions in the party had settled their differences sufficiently for Roy Jenkins to take on the role of Shadow Home Secretary in November.

The February 1974 election was called by Edward Heath as a result of the miners' dispute. Declaring the 'Who governs the country?' issue a fraud, Enoch Powell declined to seek re-election at Wolverhampton South-West. This removed any inhibitions he might have felt about encouraging Conservatives to vote Labour. At a meeting in Birmingham organized by the all-party Get Britain Out Campaign on 23 February, he delivered the first of two major campaign speeches before 1,500 people and the newsreel cameras. He said the alternative to the EEC was offered, as such alternatives must be in our parliamentary democracy, by a political party capable of securing a majority in the House of Commons:

> The entire Labour Party at this election is committed in terms of fundamental renegotiation on the Common Market, submission to the electorate—win or lose—and meanwhile a moratorium on further progress in amalgamation.
>
> There is not a single Labour candidate who has to my knowledge made a reservation on that subject. So you have a commitment which is undertaken by every section of that party, inclusive of Roy Jenkins and Michael Foot.[13]

His theme was that Britain was transferring sovereignty to a European super State and the electorate had not even been told. The Conservative manifesto omitted to mention that Britain was committed to European economic and monetary union by 1980. We had no reason to be surprised. The whole story of Britain and the Common Market to date had been one long epic of deception. The Prime Minister did not want the British people to decide at the ballot-box the most momentous transformation in their history: 'He does not think they are to be trusted with anything so important. After all they might reach the opposite conclusion to himself, and that would never do.'[14]

Because of Powell's cryptic style, stalwart Conservatives were able to leave the meeting denying that he had advised them to vote Labour.

To the best of my knowledge, Powell never used the words 'Vote Labour'. He did reveal on the eve of the election that he had used a postal vote on behalf of the Labour candidate in Wolverhampton South-West, but I do not believe he said he had voted Labour in so many words.

Labour won just four seats more than the Conservatives and was able to form a minority Government. There is evidence that Powell influenced voters, particularly in the Midlands. It is not fanciful to suggest that he won the election for Labour. The analogy he had implicitly drawn between himself and Joseph Chamberlain in 1886 was an inexact one. While he lacked Chamberlain's parliamentary following, he had more influence in the country.

James Callaghan, as Foreign Secretary, was entrusted with the renegotiation of Britain's terms of membership. Fred Peart, as Minister of Agriculture during meat and sugar crises, also had important negotiations to conduct. Because Labour lacked an overall majority in the Commons, another election was expected within a year. Labour could have kept its promise by holding an election after completing its renegotiation. But by now a referendum was in favour. We therefore heard talk that, if the renegotiation was completed in time, we might have a combined general election and referendum as had been envisaged in Harold Gurden's Bill. Electors would go to the polling-booths once to put two crosses—one for a parliamentary candidate and one for Yes or No on EEC membership. The idea was abandoned when it became evident that Wilson would ask for another election in less than a year and when President Pompidou's death and an Italian Government crisis delayed the EEC renegotiation. It was decided instead that the renegotiation could be completed within six months of the next election and a referendum held within another three months. Later it was decided to allow up to a year between election and referendum. In the event the time chosen for the referendum was June 1975, only eight months after the October 1974 election.

During the lifetime of the minority Labour Government, Jeremy Thorpe attacked the prospective referendum on new grounds. The case for holding a referendum was that a change in our system of Government needed the direct consent of the British people. Yet Harold Wilson and James Callaghan had made it clear that Britain did not want a change in the Treaty of Rome, but was concerned only with secondary matters like the Common Agricultural Policy and the size of Britain's contribution to the Community:

If for the Labour Cabinet the question of the principle of membership of the EEC is settled, can it make sense to hold a referendum about modifying technical matters? We cannot conduct budgets by referendum.[15]

This argument was confused if it was not disingenuous. It would have made sense only if there had been an earlier referendum on the EEC. In the referendum planned by the Labour Government a No vote would mean, not merely the rejection of the revised terms, but withdrawal from the EEC. The referendum would be on the principle of membership. It was simply being delayed until the best possible terms had been achieved.

A little publicized Gallup Poll in August asked: 'If the Government negotiated new terms for Britain's membership of the Common Market, and they thought it was in Britain's interests to remain a member, how would you vote then—stay in or leave it?'[16] In reply, 54 per cent said that they would vote to stay in and only 24 per cent that they would vote to leave.

The crucial question, still undecided, was whether a Labour Government would make any recommendation one way or the other. James Callaghan had said in Luxembourg in June: 'In submitting the results to the British people, we shall make clear our verdict on what has been achieved.'[17] But this assumption was questioned within the party. Harold Wilson told Robin Day on BBC1's Nationwide in August that the Cabinet might make a recommendation or it might decide to leave the issue to a free vote of the British people as a whole, in which case it was possible that members of the Cabinet would be allowed to campaign on different sides. Robin Day (like most of the British Press) thought this an extraordinary way to conduct Cabinet Government.

Despite an NEC decision to the contrary, the Labour manifesto for the October election, published on 16 September, did not commit the Cabinet to making a recommendation on EEC membership. The original draft of the manifesto promised a referendum within a year. Roy Jenkins succeeded in restoring the phrase 'through the ballot-box'—which in principle left open the possibility of a general election instead of a referendum. Since it would have meant a third election within eighteen months, however, the point seemed academic. Roy Jenkins failed to secure the deletion of a pledge that the result of a referendum would be binding on the Government.

A few days after the publication of the manifesto, Lord Chalfont resigned from the Labour Party. One of his main, if belated, reasons was that 'a popular referendum, binding upon the Government, seems to me to be in conflict with the parliamentary concept of democracy'.[18]

Lord Chalfont's resignation aroused less interest than Shirley Williams's answer at a press conference on 25 September: 'Speaking for myself I would not remain in active politics if that referendum went the wrong way from my point of view.[19] She had replied to a questioner despite Harold Wilson's attempt to restrain her.

Surprised at the excited reaction to her statement, since she did not feel she was saying anything she had not said before, Shirley Williams elaborated her views later the same day. She had not resigned from the Shadow Cabinet with Roy Jenkins because she thought that on such an important issue as the EEC the British people ought to be able to express their views in a ballot. If the Labour Cabinet advised the electorate to vote for withdrawal from the EEC, she would resign as a Minister. A majority vote in a referendum in favour of withdrawal would lead to her withdrawal from active politics: 'The fact is quite simply that I would not feel able to play a useful active role in British politics if we came out of the EEC.... There is, of course, no question whatever of my getting out of the Labour Party.'[20]

Roy Hattersley, Minister of State at the Foreign Office, immediately reasserted his pro-Market views but added that there were no conceivable circumstances in which he would either leave the Labour Party or cease to work for its success. Roy Jenkins was silent. The next day, however, he announced his support for Shirley Williams: 'I could not of course stay in a Cabinet which had to carry out a major policy which I regarded as damaging to the world and doubly so to Britain in its likely economic circumstances.'[21]

On the same day as Roy Jenkins made his statement, Harold Wilson finally succumbed to the instruction given him by the press and said it was inconceivable that the Government would fail to advise the electorate how to vote in a referendum. Dissenting members of the party would be free to express their opinions. The Whips would, however, require Labour MPs to vote in support of a Bill providing for a referendum.

Private polls showed the Labour Party that a substantial majority of electors of all the three main parties favoured a referendum. This convinced Wilson that, despite disagreements between Ministers, the EEC was a good issue for Labour. Nearer the election he declared that the Common Market had become a shambles, citing the beef and butter mountains. The question was whether the renegotiation could change all this. He accused the Conservative Government of having gone back on its pledge:

Because of the breaking of that promise the British people have never been asked to vote on the Market.

Now, after October 10 under a majority Labour Government they are going to get that chance. We will keep the promise of full-hearted consent which the Tories so brazenly broke.[22]

Heath taunted Wilson with planning a referendum which he had previously opposed. Wilson said he had been wrong then and was right now. With further cryptic support from Enoch Powell, who in this election was a successful Ulster Unionist candidate, Labour duly won an overall majority, though of only three.

After the election a small Cabinet Committee was set up to prepare for the referendum. It comprised James Callaghan, Foreign Secretary; Roy Jenkins, Home Secretary; Edward Short, Lord President of the Council; and Lord Elwyn-Jones, Lord Chancellor. Though based on departmental responsibility, the membership virtually assured that, when the renegotiation was completed, the Cabinet would advise the electorate to stay in the EEC. James Callaghan was in charge of the negotiations and was manifestly proud of what he had achieved. Roy Jenkins was the leading Labour Marketeer. Edward Short, who as Lord President was in charge of the conduct of the referendum, was a no less committed Marketeer.

A Harris poll a few weeks after the election showed that no less than 59 per cent of the public would stay in the EEC even on the existing terms. Another 15 per cent would stay in if the terms could be improved. Only 16 per cent wished to withdraw unconditionally, and there were 10 per cent 'don't knows'. These findings were dramatic. The last polls taken in 1973 had shown continuing opposition to the EEC (opposition having been predominant ever since 1967, the year when Harold Wilson first applied for membership).

Since 1973 Labour had won two elections and the Cabinet was becoming quietly reconciled to the EEC. But the public still regarded Labour as anti-Market. Moreover it had tended to blame EEC membership for Britain's unprecedented rate of inflation. The only unambiguous change since the last polls was the public's knowledge that there was to be a referendum on membership. This suggests that some of the earlier opposition to membership was displaced resentment of the way in which the Heath Government had ignored pulic opinion. The polls quoted in Chapter 1 showed a public desire for a referendum long before it became Labour policy to hold one.

The 1974 Labour Conference, postponed to the end of November because of the October election, called, by the narrow margin of 3,000,700 votes to 2,849,000, for a special party conference (which voted against EEC membership by 3,724,000 to 1,906,000 on 26 April in an Islington Sports centre). If a tired Edward Short had not referred to a 'possible referendum', Conference might have rejected the motion. The same motion demanded the right of the British Parliament to reject any EEC legislation or regulation at any time, but no one expected this to be treated seriously. By an overwhelming majority, Conference called for the referendum to be held not later than 10 October 1975; for limits on financial expenditure; and for equal publicity for pro- and anti-EEC views on television, radio and the press.

The National Referendum Campaign, formed on 7 January 1975, under the chairmanship of Neil Marten, the Conservative MP, combined the main anti-EEC organizations and parties. It was affiliated to the Anti-Common Market League (Conservative in origin), the Common

Market Safeguards Campaign (Labour in origin), Get Britain Out (Liberal in origin), Conservatives against the Treaty of Rome, British Business for World Markets, the National Council of Anti-Common Market Associations, the Scottish Nationalist Party, and the United Ulster Unionists, and was supported by trade-union leaders including Jack Jones and Clive Jenkins. Other notable anti-Marketeers were the Communist Party and the National Front.

By now the anti-Marketeers were on the defensive. The opinion polls showed support for EEC membership. A majority of the Cabinet was expected to recommend it on the renegotiated terms. Moreover, events had deprived the anti-Marketeers of arguments. They had figures to show that Britain had suffered financially from joining the EEC. Their forecast that Commonwealth markets would be lost had been vindicated. But, as James Callaghan pointed out, these lost markets could not be recovered: 'Coming out of the Market is very different from not going into the Market.'[23] Meanwhile the renegotiation was improving Britain's financial relations with other EEC members. The plan for economic and financial union by 1980 had been abandoned. The political union that was supposed to follow economic and financial union was scarcely spoken of. The restrictions on subsidies had been relaxed. In the long term the EEC might be fated to become the United States of Europe, but in the foreseeable future Britain could substantially retain its sovereignty as a member.

There had been some understanding in the Cabinet that Ministers would not engage in public controversy while the renegotiation was going on. In quick succession during January 1975 Tony Benn, Roy Hattersley and Peter Shore expressed respectively anti-EEC, pro-EEC and anti-EEC views. Harold Wilson hurriedly announced in the Commons on 23 January that the referendum would be held before the end of June, provided that the renegotiation was completed in time. The date was earlier than had been expected. Wilson had presumably decided it was best for party unity to get the referendum over as quickly as possible. The Government made its recommendation that Britain should remain in the EEC on March 18 after an EEC Heads of Government meeting in Dublin. Callaghan obtained significant improvements in the terms of Britain's membership. What improvements a Conservative Government would have obtained is an open question. The fact that a referendum was to be held on the final terms undoubtedly gave Callaghan bargaining strength. Most Marketeers (I am one) now admit that more was wrong with the original terms than they realized. A report by the European Commission in October 1974 showed that the EEC's budgetary system was unfair to Britain. Richard Norton-Taylor called the report 'an independent sanction of the Government's claim that the terms negotiated by Mr Heath imposed an unjust burden on the country'.[24] Harold Wilson understandably likes to recall the ridicule he suffered for saying the original terms were wrong. He might also recall two lines from T. S. Eliot:

> The last temptation is the greatest treason:
> To do the right deed for the wrong reason.[25]

Judged by expert hindsight, was anyone right all the time? If we accept the opinion of Wilson's colleagues that he would have accepted the same terms as Heath, none of the leading politicians showed as good judgement as public opinion. This should perplex those who opposed the referendum on the ground of public ignorance and stupidity.

7
ALIEN TO REPRESENTATIVE GOVERNMENT?

IF THE ELECTORS have more power, Parliament must have less. That the referendum is alien to representative government is a matter of definition. But how representative is our government in the first place? 'Your representative owes you, not his industry only, but his judgment; and he betrays, instead of serving you, if he sacrifices it to your opinion.'[1] Burke told his Bristol constituents this after they had elected him, which is to say that he had no mandate to ignore their opinions. A humourless Whig, Burke was conservative even in his own day. He sought to 'reconcile British superiority with American liberty'.[2] He believed in 'virtual democracy', a euphemism for disfranchisement. There was a sympathy, he believed, between MPs and the disfranchised which made virtual often better than real democracy. Let us none the less follow custom and accept Burke as the authority on British democracy. Let us judge the present House of Commons against his ideal.

Does anyone pretend that electors choose an MP for his intellect and character and thereafter let him decide for them? To discern the personal qualities of candidates on the modern hustings would require of electors more exquisite judgement than deciding for themselves whether Britain should remain in the EEC. The selection of candidates for their ability is conducted by party committees. Nor does an elected MP exercise much discretion in voting in the Commons. Free votes are rare. It was above all else the growth of party discipline which persuaded Dicey that the referendum was necessary: not only could a majority of thirty to forty attempt to introduce Home Rule; the thirty or forty probably did not believe in Home Rule anyway.[3]

Even the Government whose Whips control the majority votes is to some extent restricted by the mandate it has received. For the reality is that the elector (and in particular the floater who determines election results) votes typically for the candidate of the party whose policies he favours. He votes, that is to say, essentially on issues. The difference between an election and a referendum is between voting on a muddle of issues and on a clear one. Attlee complained that his pacifist friends thought an inefficient army less wicked than an efficient one. His paternalist friends think an inefficient democracy less wicked than an efficient one.

Governments do now seem in greater danger of defeat by their backbenchers than during the early post-war years. While this is encouraging, a number of Left-wing Labour MPs behave rebelliously because they can rely on their constituency associations to renominate them as candidates even if they incur the Leadership's displeasure. There is the danger of a new subservience against which Dick Taverne rebelled at Lincoln—and he is no longer an MP.

MPs have other allegiances, whether avowed ones, such as those to trade-union sponsors, or unavowed, such as to commercial organizations seeking (like trade unions) favourable publicity and protection of their interests. If MPs are to be bound by anyone's instructions, it should be their constituents' or their party's. Their party when in office is at least restricted by the mandate it has received from the electors.

The honest defence of our system of pseudo-representative government is that Governments are substantially free to make their own decisions, but that they make them knowing they must hold an election within five years, when the electors, if they are dissatisfied, will vote for a party with a different policy. This eschews cant about the exercise of MPs' judgement and acknowledges that the two powers in the land are electors on election day and Governments the rest of the time. The reasons we have not heard much of this argument recently are that it does not apply to more or less irrevocable issues (such as EEC membership) or to issues on which the main parties are agreed (such as EEC membership).

Those most strongly opposed to the EEC referendum on the ground that it is alien to representative Government persist in treating it as though it were not. They expressed outrage when it was suggested the Cabinet might not give a recommendation on EEC membership, and again when it was announced that the Cabinet would do so but that individual Ministers would be free to campaign against it. It was argued that the Government should resign if its recommendation was rejected by the electorate in the referendum. Every one of these arguments repudiates the fact that the referendum is alien to representative government.

There was much examination of the precedent of 1932, when Ministers in Ramsay MacDonald's National Government were allowed to express public disagreement with its protectionist policy (though not actively to campaign against it). This was despite the fact there was to be no referendum. The Anglo-Saxon tradition affords a precedent perhaps more pleasing to advocates of representative government. The Canadian Liberal Government during the Second World War was divided on a proposal to use conscripted men overseas. A plebiscite disclosed massive support for the proposal. In the event it was never implemented, but a Bill to legalize it was introduced and opposed by forty-five French Canadian MPs. 'One minister, M. Cardin, resigned from the Cabinet. The Liberal party in parliament, however, was not split because the prime minister did not make party unity a condition for his continued leadership.'⁴

The purpose of a referendum is to let a decision be taken by the electorate instead of by the Government or Parliament. The Government may make a recommendation or not as it likes. Even the Swiss Government has taken to making recommendations (to the outrage of Swiss traditionalists). The reason the Government must not resign if its recommendation is rejected was illustrated by Norway.

The Labour Government of Trygve Bratteli promised to resign if its recommendation to join the EEC was rejected. It thereby spoiled the referendum by turning it partly into a general election: anti-EEC Labour supporters tended to abstain for fear of bringing down the Government; pro-EEC Conservative supporters tended to abstain in the hope of bringing down the Government. When the Government was duly brought down, the divergent groups that had formed the opposition to the EEC experienced difficulty in forming a Government at all. The Norwegian electors manifestly wanted a Labour Government outside the EEC, and there was no good reason why they should not have had it. If in Britain a Labour recommendation to stay in the EEC was rejected by the electorate and the Government resigned, it would be succeeded, not by an anti-EEC Government, but presumably by a Conservative Government even more committed to EEC membership —which would have to negotiate the withdrawal.

Given that the Government is not going to resign if its recommendation is rejected, there is no Cabinet responsibility and no reason why Ministers should not oppose the EEC (even from the Front Bench). With all the main parties officially pro-EEC, it would have been grossly unfair to the anti-EEC case to silence, in Michael Foot and Tony Benn, two of its most articulate and influential exponents. Not the least reason for holding the referendum was that the EEC issue divided the parties. The referendum was necessary to enable both electors to vote on it and MPs and party members to campaign on it. Yet it was actually criticized on the ground that it was intended to prevent a split in the Labour Party. What, in the name of all the Irish, is the objection to that? How would it profit the country to split one of its main parties on an issue not fundamental to its creed?

In. the context of Britain's historical accession to the EEC, the arguments for representative government are academic. The leading members of the Conservative Government responsible for the accession did not rely on them. Harold Wilson, when he was earlier intending to take Britain into the EEC without a referendum, did: he was ready to say he had done lots of things the electors disagreed with at the time and this would be just one more. Reginald Maudling, on the other hand, said MPs could not disregard the views of the electors on the EEC, and Edward Heath implied that Britain ought not to join without the full-hearted consent of its Parliament and people.

ELECTORS' INCOMPETENCE?

The original reason for allowing MPs to become representatives instead of delegates was geographical. The early MPs did not have time to ride home to consult constituents in the West and North before casting their votes. Modern communications have removed this reason. It would be possible for electors to watch Commons debates on television and cast their own votes electronically at the end. The case for the MP as representative now rests on the specialized knowledge required in Government. As Clifford Sharp argued,[5] this does not imply intellectual superiority on the part of MPs. If MPs were chosen by lot, they would soon know far more about politics than their constituents. Perhaps the ideal of representative government is that an MP should vote, not as his constituents wish, but as they would wish if they had his knowledge.

One argument put against the EEC referendum was that only a dozen people in the country were capable of understanding all the economic implications. If this were true, not only the electorate but Parliament would be disqualified from voting on it. This argument can indeed be used to defend the modern party discipline which effectively leaves decisions to a Government acting on the specialized and experienced advice provided by the civil service.

There is something in these arguments, and reasonable men may disagree about how decision-making should be distributed among Ministers, MPs and electors. But the degree of paternalism in twentieth-century Britain is, like bullfighting, something which no one could regard as normal without having been brought up on it. Governments keep, not only power, but information to themselves. We know from the Crossman diaries[6] that even junior Cabinet Ministers have to accept that it is better they should not be told about affairs of state. A good Minister in the Commons means now, not one who answers questions well, but one who evades them well. As to the electors, it is even suggested that they should not be allowed to know how they themselves vote: the votes in the EEC referendum are not to be counted by constituency lest it be disclosed that MPs' views are different from their constituents' (which shows no belief in representative government). Saddest of all is the way electors dutifully reply to the pollsters that they are not competent to say whether Britain should remain in the EEC. Britain could give the Soviet Union lessons in brainwashing.

British correspondents reporting the campaign for the Italian referendum on divorce in May 1974 took the view that the electors' ignorance made it a farce: many electors did not even know Italy had a divorce law, let alone what it said or how many people had been granted divorces under it. This was a condemnation, not of the referendum, but of the representative government that had preceded it. It was representative government that had kept the electors ignorant. It was the referendum campaign—the need to win their votes—which enabled them to learn about the divorce law. In the end there was little doubt that they succeeded in casting informed votes. In general British electors are better educated and more sophisticated than Italian. If we allow a referendum only on a Bill that has been debated in Parliament, the electors will be informed about its subject-matter even before the referendum campaign begins. There is no need to hold a referendum on the complexities of VAT.

So long as the Government is the judge in its own case, it will assume that most affairs of state are too difficult to bother the people with. EEC membership was certainly never too difficult. Under representative government, the electors were deceived at the time of Britain's accession into thinking that it was simply an economic issue. They did not realize it meant an initial loss of sovereignty and the likelihood of progressive federalism during the years ahead.

The Marketeers are still seeking to confuse the issue. But I imagine that before the referendum campaign is finished the electors will know essentially what they have to decide: are they prepared to forgo something of their British separateness and to make some short-term economic sacrifices in order that in the long term they may enjoy greater political power and prosperity as Europeans? This is not something anyone else can tell them. It is a matter of personal preference. A referendum is the best way of deciding the issue. The only objection to it is that future generations, whose interests are involved, do not get a vote. The intellectual effort required of electors is far less than that required of jurymen. If electors were incapable of making it, the British system of justice would be indefensible.

REACTIONARY INFLUENCE?

The referendum was proposed by the Conservatives in 1910-11 as a veto on legislation. While in principle it is possible to veto reactionary legislation, it is understandable that Labour envisaged the referendum as an impediment to progress. In addition the mass of electors were felt to be suspicious of change—which is a special aspect of electors' alleged incompetence.

The subject invariably quoted in this context is capital punishment. MPs abolished it in a free vote when the opinion polls showed the electorate in favour of it. The polls have continued to show the electorate in favour of it.

Let us examine the evidence of Switzerland, which we know has the most extensive experience of referenda. Capital punishment was abolished in Zurich as early as 1867. It was abolished throughout Switzerland by a new Federal Constitution in 1874 but was reintroduced in 1879 by eight cantons and one of the half-cantons (there being twenty-two cantons in all). It was finally abolished in the Swiss Penal Code of 1937 which came into force after a federal referendum in 1942 (except that the Swiss Military Penal Code retains shooting in wartime). The last execution for a criminal offence was in 1940.

Opinions recorded by the British pollsters are pub talk, in the literal sense irresponsible. Many abolitionist MPs believed in capital punishment until they became MPs and found themselves with responsibility for hanging people. The chairman of the Royal Commission which recommended the abolition of capital punishment believed in it until his role required him to examine the evidence. If ever we had a referendum on capital punishment, MPs and the media would educate the electorate about it, and the electorate, finding itself with power over life and death, would have a reason for listening. The only way to make electors or anyone else behave responsibly is to give them responsibility.

A Swiss referendum on a different subject affords more precise evidence of this process. Switzerland was the only country to hold (in 1920) a referendum on joining the League of Nations. All the Federal Councillors were in favour of joining. The National Council voted in favour by 128 to 43, the Council of States by 33 to 6. None the less the Swiss Councillors felt that the decision whether to join the League should be put to referendum. Partly this was because it affected national sovereignty. Partly it was because of strong popular opposition to joining. The farming community appeared to take exception to the fact that the League was foreign. The socialists regarded it as capitalist. Swiss of all backgrounds and beliefs felt it would prejudice their country's traditional neutrality: the exclusion of Germany and Russia made it look like a war victors' club—except that the reluctance of the United States to join made it look even less international. Undoubtedly influenced by the referendum, the Council of the League, out of deference to Switzerland's neutrality, provided that it need take part only in economic, not military, sanctions, and that it need not allow the transit of foreign troops for operations against an aggressor nation. The Swiss voted to join, though the necessary majority of the cantons was only just obtained.

'One big advantage of the referendum in Switzerland,' wrote Georg Thürer, 'is that it encourages this sort of open debate and acts as a political safety valve, ensuring that criticism is not driven underground'.[7] In Britain the opposition to the EEC registered by the polls changed after the referendum was announced. This was surely due less to the renegotiation than to a more responsible attitude and to removal of resentment that Parliament had manifestly disregarded public opinion.

Dicey wrote: 'It is to innovators or reformers, at least, as much as to Conservatives, that the Referendum should commend itself. Unwarranted innovation produces revolutionary reaction.'[8] We see this over capital punishment. Resentment at Parliament's disregard of public opinion continues. It is largely responsible for periodical demands for its restoration. Moreover, MPs are not such fervent believers in representative government that they ignore such resentment. There are many measures of penal reform they refrain from advocating for fear of alienating public opinion further. After the Birmingham bombings in 1974, Julian Critchley, a Conservative MP previously opposed to capital punishment, gave the following reason for restoring it for terrorists:

Punishment may not be a valid or effective answer to terrorism, although its imposition must deter somewhat, but unless the public be permitted a catharsis, an act of revenge if you like, an opportunity to express its disapproval at indiscriminate killing and maiming, we may rupture the links between people and Parliament, bonds that have already been loosened.[9]

This is to abandon representative government without substituting direct democracy. It is to drag Parliament down to the level of the electors' ignorance instead of using a referendum to raise the electors to Parliament's enlightenment. The whole argument may be reduced to mathematics. On a scale of progressiveness, representative government has Parliament (P_1) slightly ahead of a reactionary electorate (E_1). The use of referenda gets them approximately level $(P_2=E_2)$. If $E_2>P_1$, then $P_2>P_1$, and the use of referenda is making for more progressive legislation. This is why the referendum does not have to be a reactionary influence even when used only as a veto on legislation. The enlightenment of the electorate for which the referendum is responsible gives Parliament the confidence to pass more progressive legislation in the first place.

DEMAGOGUERY

It is the plebiscite, as distinct from the constitutional referendum, which gives scope for demagoguery. The demagogues closely associated with referenda have been Napoleon I, Napoleon III, Hitler and de Gaulle. Of these only de Gaulle experienced the restrictions of the constitutional referendum, which in the event brought about his downfall. The other three were not even restricted by effective democracy. In the plebiscites that appointed Napoleon Consul for life in 1802, voting was by the system of signing public registers. If a demagogue can make his own rules, he can exploit the referendum. If he can make his own rules, however, he can lead a depraved political life without the referendum. The referendum is an effect rather than a cause of populist government.

West Germany remains understandably suspicious of referenda, but the circumstances created by the Weimar Republic are unlikely ever to be repeated. The framers of the Weimar Constitution feared the power of party bureaucracies, particularly in a *Reichstag* of inexperienced parliamentarians. It was as a safeguard against this real danger that they chose to give the people a share in government by means of the referendum, the initiative, and the direct election of the *Reich* President. Having created the alternative danger of demagoguery, they compounded it by making the President Supreme Commander of the Army and by empowering him to use the Army for the restoration of law and order and, in an emergency, to suspend most of the constitutional liberties, including *habeas corpus*.

The Weimar Constitution prepared the way for a *Führer*, but not without help. Max Weber, largely responsible for Article 41 ('The President of the *Reich* is elected by the whole German people'), expounded the theory of the mystical character of a leader acclaimed by the ritual of a popular vote. The German people, after suffering defeat and deprivation, were peculiarly susceptible to aggressive romanticism.

A constitutional Head of State with no share in government, as in Britain or the French Fourth Republic, is a safeguard against demagoguery. The Fifth Republic broke with French Republican tradition and exalted the President. Its Constitution was designed for de Gaulle. It created an executive Presidency without the checks and balances of the United States Constitution. The Assembly was given as little power as an early English Parliament. Surprisingly, in view of its populist inception, the original Constitution of the Fifth Republic did not provide for the direct election of the President. De Gaulle was a patrician, even an aloof, demagogue. Direct election was introduced later.

The demagogue uses the referendum to make, not decisions, but propaganda. The essential technique, perfected by Hitler, is to concentrate people's attention on real or imaginary dangers while suggesting that he and he alone can overcome them. De Gaulle and the French Right benefited in the 1968 elections from spontaneous fears aroused by the 'May revolution'. Where, however, de Gaulle needed to explain the dangers—of British domination of the EEC, or of American domination of French industry—he proved too aloof a demagogue either to create panic or to suggest that he had the solution.

At the fifth referendum held under the Fifth Republic, on 27 April 1969, French electors were asked:

Do you approve the Bill submitted to the French people by the President of the Republic concerning the creation of regions and the renovation of the Senate?

Perversely de Gaulle determined to make this referendum a vote of confidence in himself. He declared that he would resign if the electorate did not support the Bill. When it rejected it by a narrow majority, he was as good as his word.

It is also feared that referenda may give scope to demagogues who are not (or not yet) the Government. Cal McCrystal described the scope given by the Norwegian EEC referendum to the political 'crazies':

These campaigners persuaded many Norwegians that a Yes vote would send hordes of swarthy Latins rushing up the fjords to rape Norwegian women; that untrustworthy men with sand in their hair and tar on their boots would steal the best lumberjack jobs; that the Pope would undermine the nation's strong Lutheran traditions ('If Norway enters the kingdom of the anti-Christ', went one warning, 'thousands will fall into the devil's net'); that the whole place would be swamped with booze; that there would be a brain-drain to Germany, but that the Germans would then buy up all the choice sites in Norwegian lakeside resorts; that once the Mediterranean predators had finished raping, they would open dozens of brothels; and that bicycles would be banned from the streets of Oslo.[10]

We may accept that all this was said while questioning that it was believed. It is true the Norwegians elected to stay out of the EEC, but Cal McCrystal himself observed that the Marketeers left their campaign too late. Moreover the fishermen and farmers had good commercial reasons for staying out, and Norway is in fact prospering.

In Britain liberals think with horror of the scope a referendum on immigration would give to Enoch Powell. They would do better to dwell on the scope given him by the present system. In 1968 the anti-immigration movement led by Powell and Duncan Sandys inspired the Labour Government to pass the Commonwealth Immigration Act in a single week. The Government was so frightened of Enoch Powell it was not deterred by the fact that fifteen Conservative as well as thirty-five Labour MPs voted against the Bill, let alone by reasoned arguments about its dishonourable character and evil effects. The knowledge that a Bill could be put to referendum—that the buck could be passed to the people—would surely have persuaded the Government to act less precipitately and illiberally.

When the Conservative Government admitted Ugandan Asians expelled by President Amin, the Labour Party Front Bench kept quiet, presumably for fear of offending working-class racialists. British liberals have said little in public about immigration, whether from fear or from the belief, inspired by representative government, that good must be done by stealth. Enoch Powell was allowed a public monopoly of the subject.

A referendum on immigration would force liberals not only to talk

about other people's prejudices, but to discover other people's realities
—for, though skin colour does not make a man any different, the fact
that he comes from a different country and culture does. When English-
men are moved to another part of England under 'overspill schemes',
the need to induct them into their new environment is acknowledged.
Yet virtually nothing is done to induct people coming from abroad. A
referendum campaign would help to draw attention to such absurdities
and might lead to a rational immigration policy such as the Dutch have.
No doubt some unpleasant emotions would be displayed, as during the
campaign for the Norwegian EEC referendum. But the referendum
would release, not create, these emotions. The moral is that Britain,
like Norway, has held too few referenda in the past.

APATHY

We have considered the objection that referenda turn electors into
hysterical automatons trooping to the polls to say Yea or Nay at
the Leader's behest. At the other extreme is the objection that the
demands of referenda produce an electorate of rational cynics too
bored to go to the polls at anyone's behest.

The holding of referenda need not consume any time at all. Harold
Gurden wanted referenda held with general elections. That is to say,
an elector would go to the polling-station to vote for a Conservative,
Labour or Liberal candidate, and at the same time would vote for or
against restricting immigration. This would be acceptable only if an
election and a referendum needed to be held at about the same time.
One advantage of a referendum is that it enables electors to express
an opinion without the disruption of a general election. This would be
wasted if a referendum was deferred until the next election.

There should be provision to render invalid a result determined by
apathy. A requirement for a majority of 55 per cent or some higher
figure would be inadequate since it would not prevent an issue from
being determined by a low poll. The Temperance (Scotland) Act 1913
provided for Limitation to be carried by a bare majority provided that
those in favour constituted at least 35 per cent of the registered electors.
This is a better principle, though we might adopt a figure of a third
(or 33⅓ per cent) as being easier to remember.

We must not adopt the other principle of the 1913 Act, that, where
the 35 per cent is wanting, the *status quo* shall be preserved. This is
suitable for constitutional amendments, where the intention is to make
change difficult. To apply it to ordinary Bills would be to defer to
apathy and to make the referendum a force for conservatism. It would
be analogous to having a House of Commons in which it was always
possible that MPs would be too lazy or preoccupied to form a quorum.

The intention is to provide a safeguard against apathy. Where the
winning votes are less than a third of the registered electors, Parliament

must be free to proceed as though there had been no referendum. If the electorate is not concerned to veto a Bill, Parliament can pass it. Where Rousseauesque democracy fails, representative democracy shall prevail.

It is interesting that Denmark has provision to treat referenda in both ways. A referendum on a Bill passed by the *Folketing* must be held at the request of one-third of all MPs. It is rejected if opposed by a majority of those voting and 30 per cent of all electors. Otherwise it becomes law. A constitutional amendment becomes law only when there has been an election and it has been passed by the new *Folketing*, and when it has also been put to referendum and supported by a majority of those voting and by 40 per cent of all electors.

GOVERNMENT'S POSITION AFTER REJECTION OF ITS POLICY

Suppose that a Government's recommendation is rejected in a referendum. Even though it be entitled to remain in office, will it not lack authority? This exercised Churchill when (as a Liberal) he opposed the Conservative proposal for referenda on 'constitutional amendments' in 1911.

Balfour recalled in reply that Governments were always dropping Bills because of pressure in the Commons. A major one dropped in recent years was the earlier Wilson Government's Industrial Relations Bill, because of opposition by trade unions and its own backbenchers. This was a Bill to which the Government was fully committed. Its withdrawal surely involved more loss of authority than would the rejection in a referendum of a recommendation on the EEC, a subject on which the Labour Government itself made a reluctant and pragmatic judgement. Surely the Heath Government lost more authority in committing Britain to membership of the EEC at a time when the opinion polls showed the electors to be opposed to it. There is a closer analogy. Governments sometimes make recommendations in free votes in the Commons and suffer no loss of authority if they are rejected. How did Harold Wilson persuade himself that he needed majority support for EEC membership in the Parliamentary Labour Party?

Electors voted Labour in October 1974 on the understanding that the Government would be bound by the referendum result. If the result should be NO, the Government would be not merely entitled but obliged to stay in office. Both honour and British tradition would require it to fulfil its mandate by negotiating Britain's withdrawal from the EEC.

8
ALIEN TO THE BRITISH CONSTITUTION?

ATTLEE THOUGHT THE referendum alien to British traditions. More recently Peter Jenkins wrote of Labour's foolish commitment to this 'alien device'[1] and Norman St John-Stevas spoke of it as this 'nasty continental aberration'.[2] Addressing the other EEC Foreign Ministers, an alien audience to whom the referendum was familiar, James Callaghan could not bring himself to use the word. He spoke of testing British opinion either by a general election or by 'another method'[3] (as though the referendum was as alien as the House of Lords).

We have held more local referenda than we can count, plus the first of a series in Northern Ireland. We nearly held national referenda on the Parliament Act and Empire Free Trade. Dicey advocated one on Home Rule and Churchill one on the prolongation of the Coalition. Moreover, the Conservative Party wanted the referendum permanently substituted for the Lords' veto. If the referendum is incompatible with British institutions, the grounds must be theoretical, not historical.

When Dicey advocated a referendum on Home Rule, he was seeking to compensate for the British Constitution's lack of 'entrenched clauses' —laws that cannot be altered as easily as ordinary laws. An amendment to the United States Constitution can be passed only by three-quarters of the States. Home Rule, changing not merely the Constitution but the territory of the United Kingdom could have been passed, in the same way as a Licensing Act, by simple majorities in both Houses. In 1911 the Conservative Party was seeking to entrench basic features of the Constitution by providing that they should not be amended without a majority in a referendum. This would have meant a fundamental change in the British Constitution. But the Parliament Act 1911 did in any case leave the British Constitution with one entrenched clause. The House of Lords could no longer veto any Bill except one to prolong the lifetime of Parliament. That the maximum lifetime of Parliament is five years thus became, and remains, an entrenched clause. To alter it a Government ought first to obtain a mandate at a general election or in a referendum. Then, unless the Lords respected the electors' wishes to the extent of willingly sacrific-

74

ing its own power, the Government would have to ask the Sovereign for the creation of more peers.

Dicey is associated with the dictum that no British Parliament can commit its successors.[4] This was invoked by Harold Wilson in 1971 as justification for asking to renegotiate Britain's terms of entry to the EEC.[5] Mark Arnold-Forster argued from it in *The Guardian* that a referendum was necessary to give the EEC a guarantee that Britain would remain a member.

> If no Parliament can bind its successor then no Parliament can abolish the principle that no Parliament can bind its successor. Someone else, the sovereign people, for example would have to do the job itself.[6]

I am reluctant to forgo an argument in favour of the referendum, particularly one so elegant as this. Moreover, I am sympathetic to the concept of the sovereign people. But it is a Saxon or Swiss concept connoting the delegation of power upwards. It is itself alien to the British Constitution. It is denied by the concept of parliamentary sovereignty and cannot therefore be invoked to complement it.

Dr E. C. S. Wade, the editor of Dicey's *Law of the Constitution*, allowed in a footnote[7] that Parliament may transfer sovereignty, but defines any body to which sovereignty is transferred as a successor. Thus, when a British Parliament transfers some of its sovereignty to the EEC, future British Parliaments and the EEC authorities become co-successors. The British Parliament does not thereby commit its successors. It does, however, commit future British Parliaments.

All this is needlessly subtle. The plain fact is that British Parliaments have often committed their successors. The present British Parliament could not invoke Dicey's dictum in order to rescind Indian Independence or to start dropping bombs on past enemy countries with which previous British Parliaments had negotiated peace treaties. The reason it is possible for Britain to withdraw from the EEC has nothing to do with the British Constitution. It is that EEC membership, unlike Indian Independence, is not of its nature entirely irrevocable. Britain is neither more nor less free to withdraw from the EEC than its other members with their different Constitutions and Parliaments.

Jennings gave as an example of the sovereignty of the British Parliament that it could pass a Bill forbidding smoking in the streets of Paris.[8] That Frenchmen would disobey it was, he argued, by the way, since the sovereignty of Parliament was a legal fiction. What is not by the way is that the British Parliament acknowledges at least some international law. The British Parliament would deny that it had the right to rescind Indian Independence or to drop bombs on ex-enemy countries. To this extent the sovereignty of Parliament is not even a legal fiction.

At the same time Mark Arnold-Forster is manifestly right in suggesting that other members of the EEC would be reassured about Britain's continuing membership if it was endorsed in a referendum. Not only would it mean that the British themselves regarded the issue as settled. It would imply that, if ever in changed circumstances Britain should wish to withdraw, the Government would again feel that it needed the consent, not only of Parliament, but also of the people in a referendum. It would make of Britain's EEC membership an implicit entrenched clause.

All Dicey meant in saying that no British Parliament could commit its successors was that the Constitution had no entrenched clauses. A British Parliament could in fact have committed its successors at any time by introducing entrenched clauses as Dicey and the Conservative Party wished. It could even now pass an Act saying that Britain should never withdraw from the EEC without majority approval in a referendum. It could also, again as Dicey and the Conservative Party wished, entrench clauses involving no international commitment, such as the Protestant Succession and the distribution of seats. In so far as it is true that a British Parliament cannot commit its successors, it cannot commit itself either.

British Parliaments have bound both themselves and their successors even in respect of ordinary legislation. The Parliament Act 1911 provided that an ordinary Bill rejected by the Lords could be passed only after two years' delay. The Labour Party declared in its 1945 election manifesto that 'we will not tolerate obstruction of the people's will by the House of Lords'. The Parliament Act 1949 reducing the Lords' delaying power to one year was delayed by the Lords for two years.

During the debate on the report stage of the Northern Ireland Constitution Act 1973, Richard Mitchell, the Labour MP, objected to the promise of future referenda on the Border (as distinct from objecting to the referenda themselves) on the ground that 'the Bill, or any pledge given by the Secretary of State or by the Opposition Front Bench, cannot bind a future Parliament'.[9] John Biggs-Davison, the Conservative MP, replied:

> The hon. Member for Southampton, Itchen, (Mr R. C. Mitchell) said, correctly, that whatever we do, however we legislate, we cannot bind our successors. That was true, presumably, of the Labour Government when they enacted the 1949 Act which stipulated that there would be no change in the status of Northern Ireland without the consent of the Parliament of Northern Ireland.[10]

The only tenable objection to the promise of future Border referenda was that the Conservative Government did not have a mandate to give it. It would be wrong for a British Parliament to give the Lords the power to put a Bill to referendum unless the governing party had a mandate to do so. Once the Lords had been given the power, it would be wrong for Parliament to take it away unless again the governing party had been given a mandate to do so. The power of the Lords to put a Bill to referendum would not differ in constitutional principle from its present power to delay a Bill for a year.

If there is an aspect of the British system to which the referendum is alien, it is its strict party discipline. This derives from the right of the British Prime Minister to ask the Sovereign for a dissolution— that is for a general election—when his Government is defeated on a vote of confidence. Rebellious Government backbenchers face the prospect of being put out of work. The instability of the French Third Republic was attributed to the fact that MPs could defeat a Government without fear of a general election. Holding referenda in Britain would not in principle be different from allowing MPs free votes. In practice it could reduce the number of issues treated as votes of confidence and give Parliament as well as people some power over Governments between elections. We may have reached the point where this can fairly be regarded as un-British.

GOVERNMENT'S WEAKNESS IN NEGOTIATIONS

It is alleged that the Government's authority is weakened in international negotiations if it must put any agreement it signs to referendum. This presupposes that, because of strict party discipline, ratification by Parliament can be taken for granted. In practice the Government may feel obliged to allow a free vote, or, if the issue is important enough, MPs may defy the Whip. Despite the Conservative majority, it was uncertain to the end whether the Commons would pass the European Communities Bill.

Moreover, the Government lacked authority after the passing of the Bill. The opinion polls showed British opposition to membership. Labour declared that when returned to office it would reopen negotiations and subsequently hold a referendum unless the Conservatives held one first. The Irish, Danish and Norwegian representatives negotiating with the EEC had not appeared to lack prestige or bargaining power because their agreements would be subject to referenda. After the Irish and Danish electorates had voted in favour of membership, their Governments were able to speak on European matters with far greater authority than Edward Heath. Robert Stephens, *The Observer's* diplomatic correspondent, wrote before the October 1974 election:

So it is arguable that only when a Labour Government has approved terms for British membership and secured popular endorsement for them will there be any real stability in Britain's

77

relations with Europe and an open road for the Community's future evolution.[11]

We have seen that, when James Callaghan undertook the renegotiation of Britain's terms of membership, the prospect of a referendum among a hostile electorate significantly increased his bargaining power—just as it had that of the Swiss Government *vis-à-vis* the League of Nations in 1920.

The point is worth making that the arguments both for and against referenda may apply to domestic as well as to international negotiations. Suppose that an Industrial Relations Bill was to be put to referendum. The need to secure ratification by the electorate as well as by Parliament would make the Government less able to commit itself in negotiations with the TUC. But, since the Conservatives found that an Industrial Relations Act need not be obeyed merely because it has been passed, popular approval in a referendum, effectively rebutting accusations of capitalist oppression, would ultimately increase the Government's authority.

9
IMPROPER INFLUENCES

PHRASING THE QUESTION

THE ULTIMATE LEADING question makes use of the limited option patented at Hyde Park Corner:

Why don't you stop beating your wife?
Why is Harry Pollitt a Chinaman?

The limited option has appeared in some opinion polls and in theory a Government could use it in a referendum:

Do you think income tax should be 98p or 99p in the pound?

Do you think the punishment for income-tax evasion should be fourteen years' or fifteen years' imprisonment?

This prospect need not frighten us. No Government would conduct such a referendum unless it was already an effective dictatorship. We are concerned with the use of the referendum in a democratic society. Even so, may not the phrasing of the question determine the answers given? Condorcet told the National Convention in 1793 that, to avoid this danger, only 'simple propositions'[1] should be put. Here then is a simple proposition:

Do you wish that Italy shall remain what it is now—a collection of petty States each afraid of its neighbours, or else that it shall be a great kingdom united under one great king?

That, according to W. H. Mallock in *The Limits of Pure Democracy*,[2] is the question in the plebiscite which established the dynasty of Victor Emmanuel. It is too good to be true, or Mallock's translation too free to be accurate. The authoritative version is tendentious enough. The voters of Naples and Sicily were required in 1860 to say Yes or No to the proposition:

The people wish Italy one and indivisible with Vittorio Emmanuele as their Constitutional King and his legitimate descendants after him.[3]

A modern opinion poll got opposite results according to whether it

79

asked, 'Do you wish this country to join the Common Market?' or 'Do you wish to see a United Europe of which this country would form a part?' Nor is tendentiousness the only problem. Even without Machiavellian intent, a question may be recondite, ambiguous, misleading or confusing. The pollsters have innumerable examples of different results induced by slight changes of wording. While all this is impressive evidence of the dangers of opinion polls, it has no bearing on referenda in a modern democratic society.

Suppose that six months before a general election the pollsters presented electors with the names of their prospective candidates and required them to say how they would vote. Analysis would no doubt show that replies depended upon the order in which candidates' names were presented. They would afford massive evidence of voters' incompetence, indeed of the inadvisability of leaving the election of MPs to ordinary citizens. Yet all is well on polling day. By then there has been an election campaign. An elector has both decided which party he wishes to vote for and learned the name of that party's candidate. Candidates' parties are now indicated on ballot-papers, but electors managed to vote purposefully even when they were not.

So it is with a referendum. The returning officer does not, like a pollster, ask the elector a question without warning. Nor does the elector go to the polling-booth and read the question to find out what it is all about. Before polling day there has been a campaign, during which he has heard the evidence and made up his mind. The fact that he goes to the polling-booth means he wishes to vote, which means he knows how he intends to vote. His mind is fully made up before ever he reads the question. If he is convinced by the Marketeers and the Marketeers say vote Yes, he may well vote without ever reading the question. If there is any chance of his marking his ballot-paper wrongly by mistake, the politicians will have drawn his attention to it as they do when two Smiths stand against one another in the same constituency.

The 1974 Italian referendum on divorce should have put an end to arguments based on the phrasing of the question. The Italian electors are less sophisticated than the British. Many did not know Italy already had a divorce law, let alone what it said. Commentators forecast that the referendum question (without being tendentious) would mislead them:

Do you want Law No. 898 of 1 December 1970—Norms on the Dissolution of Marriage—to be abrogated?

This was the law which had introduced divorce under the Italian State. Electors who were against divorce needed to vote Yes, those who were for it to vote No. Moreover the Italian *abrogazione* is as difficult a word as its English equivalent. In an 86 per cent poll the unsophisticated

Italian electors none the less succeeded in voting as they wanted. This may be inferred from the geographical distribution of the votes. The sixty-six of Italy's ninety-four provinces which went to the divorce-law abolitionists were for the most part rural areas or other areas where Catholicism was known to be strong.

The White Paper on the *Referendum on United Kingdom Membership of the European Community*[4] a question to which the Referendum Bill added '(the Common Market)':

> The Government have announced the results of the renegotiation of the United Kingdom's terms of membership of the European Community.
> DO YOU THINK THAT THE UNITED KINGDOM SHOULD STAY IN THE EUROPEAN COMMUNITY?
>
> YES ☐
> NO ☐

Critics persuaded themselves, on the evidence of a National Opinion Poll, that 'stay in' was tendentious and gave the Marketeers an 8.6 per cent advantage over asking whether the United Kingdom should 'come out of' the European Community. It would have been possible to ask: 'Do you think that the United Kingdom should be in the European Community (the Common Market)?' The alternative considered seems to have been to model the ballot-paper on that in the Northern Ireland referendum, itself inspired by an earnest desire to avoid tendentiousness:

> Do you think that the United Kingdom should stay in the European Community (the Common Market)?
>
> Do you think that the United Kingdom should come out of the European Community (the Common Market)?

The discretion in the wording arises because the EEC referendum is a plebiscite. If Britain had held a constitutional referendum on the European Communities Bill in 1972, there would have been a predetermined form as neutral, though not necessarily as obscure, as that in the Italian referendum on divorce. If the proposals in Balfour of Burleigh's Bill[5] had been followed, electors would have been instructed:

If you wish the Bill, the short title of which is 'European Communities Bill' to become law, place a cross under the word 'Yes'. If not, place a cross under the word 'No'.	YES	NO

A simpler form is possible:

Are you in favour of the European Communities Bill?

This is not very different from the basic question put in the library referenda:

Are you in favour of the adoption of the Public Libraries Act, 1892, for the borough of so-and-so?[6]

In a referendum on a Bill there is a case for including information about the parliamentary process:

Are you in favour of the European Communities Bill which has been passed by the House of Commons and the House of Lords?

On occasion the information would be different:

Are you in favour of such-and-such a Bill which has been passed by the House of Commons but rejected by the House of Lords?

Perhaps we cannot rely on Governments to give Bills neutral titles when referenda are a possibility. Perhaps, if the constitutional referendum had been introduced before 1972, we should never have heard of a European Communities Bill and electors would have been asked:

Are you in favour of the Bill to Enable Britain to be No Longer Excluded from the Great United Europe in which Lie her Destiny and Prosperity?

Something of the kind has happened in Australia, where federal referenda are held on all constitutional amendments. The neutral (or relatively neutral) short titles of amendments are not used on the ballot-papers. Here is part of a ballot-paper referring to an amendment entitled Constitution Alteration (Democratic Elections) 1974:

An Act to alter the Constitution so as to ensure that the Members of the House of Representatives and of the Parliaments of the States are chosen directly and democratically by the People. DO YOU APPROVE the proposed law?'

I have suggested that Britain should have an independent Referendum Commission by analogy with the Boundary Commission. Not the least of its functions would be to pronounce on the wording of questions, including the titles of Bills included in them. A Government that defied the Commission's advice would condemn itself. The most likely form of abuse is for a Government to include two or more different questions in a single referendum. The referendum that brought about de Gaulle's downfall in 1969 asked:

Do you approve the Bill submitted to the French people by the

President of the Republic concerning the creation of regions and the renovation of the Senate?

Whatever the result of this referendum had been, no one would have known whether there was a majority either for regionalization or for Senate reform. It is believed that the Prime Minister, Couve de Murville, wanted the two questions separated out in the referendum (which would have required two Bills), but that de Gaulle would not consent. Since he was making the referendum a question of confidence, it was immaterial to de Gaulle whether the electors rejected one or both. Perhaps he felt that giving them the opportunity to vote on the two separately would encourage them to reject one or the other.

In another referendum held on the same day as the one already referred to, the Australian electorate rejected a constitutional amendment entitled 'Constitutional Alteration (MODE OF ALTERING THE CONSTITUTION) 1974'. This would have given votes in future referenda on constitutional amendments to the 130,700 electors in the Australian Capital Territory and Northern Territory, who are disfranchised by the fact that the Constitution allows votes in referenda only to electors 'in each State'. The same constitutional amendment would have made future constitutional amendments valid if approved by majorities of the electors in only half the States instead of in a majority of them (in three instead of four). The Labor Government wanted to make it easier to pass constitutional amendments. It put a controversial proposal to achieve this end together with one of self-evident justice, the enfranchisement in referenda of the electors in the Territories. It presumably hoped a popular desire to see justice done would carry the other half of the amendment. Instead a popular reluctance to make it easier to pass constitutional amendments had the incidental effect of maintaining the disfranchisement of electors in the Territories. Again we should look to the Referendum Commission for protection. If it felt a Bill dealt with two separate subjects, it could ask that certain clauses be taken out and presented in a separate Bill.

I have taken two examples of suspect referenda from Australia. It is fair to add that Australia makes frequent and excellent use of the referendum. (Voting in referenda, as in elections, is compulsory.) It is because there are so many Australian referenda to choose from that one can find examples of most things. The two separate Australian referenda I have referred to were held on the same day and the questions appeared on the same ballot-paper. The ballot-paper in fact showed four separate constitutional amendments to which electors were required to say Yes or No. It is common in both Australia and Switzerland to hold several referenda at once. In the Republic of Ireland in 1972 electors were asked on the same day to say separately whether the Catholic Church should lose its special position under the Constitution and whether the voting age should be lowered from twenty-one to eighteen. While there is much to be said for saving electors journeys to the polling-stations, there must be reservations about holding more than two referenda on the same day. It is difficult to conduct satisfactory campaigns for several referenda simultaneously. If half a dozen referenda are held on the same day, electors may perhaps be influenced by the phrasing of the questions or simply cast their votes in a lacklustre and uninformed manner. Perhaps Australian and Swiss voters have acquired the necessary sophistication over the years, but it is not a practice to be recommended for beginners.

UNEQUAL PUBLICITY

Holding referenda only on Bills that have been debated in Parliament, and hence reported and discussed in the media, is some guarantee that electors will be informed about the issues. Is there not none the less a danger that one point of view will secure a disproportionate amount of publicity? This danger does not arise if the main parties are opposed on an issue. If, however, the Labour, Conservative and Liberal Party Leaderships all recommend that Britain should remain in the EEC, are not the anti-Marketeers put at a disadvantage?

In so far as they are at a disadvantage, this is because they have already lost the argument within their own parties. Anti-Marketeers must get far more publicity with a referendum than without one. By 1975, if the issue had been resolved by representative government— by a vote in the Commons—the anti-Marketeers would have had no chance at all. In Britain in particular, a referendum immediately assures both points of view fair time on television and radio. The White Paper suggested the Government would follow the example of Norway and Denmark in giving financial assistance to organizations campaigning both for and against EEC membership. Norway, with a population of less than four million, disbursed about £815,000 in this way, and Denmark, with one of five million, about £1.4m.

If one side is much richer than the other, equal financial help (as envisaged in the White Paper) will be far more valuable to the poorer. There can be some difficulty in deciding how the money should be distributed among different campaigning organizations. If we introduced the constitutional referendum, this could be made the responsibility of the Referendum Commission.

The Commission could also be given the responsibility, accepted by many Governments in countries where referenda are held, of sending electors information about the issues. The ballot-paper in the Republic of Ireland's referendum on joining the EEC simply asked (both in Gaelic and English) if the elector approved of the proposal in the Third Amendment to the Constitution Bill 1974. It did not say what the proposal was. But every elector received a polling-card which gave the Third Amendment in full (not easy reading) and followed it by a short explanatory paragraph: 'The purpose of the proposal is to allow the State to become a member of the communities commonly known as the European Communities.' This may be regarded as the provision of minimum information. At the other extreme, Swiss electors are liable to receive a short book on a referendum. In Australia, when referenda are to be held on constitutional amendments, the Commonwealth Government publishes a

PAMPHLET CONTAINING

ARGUMENTS IN FAVOUR of the Proposed Laws authorized by a majority of the Members of the Parliament who voted for the Proposed Laws and desire to forward such arguments;

and

ARGUMENTS AGAINST the Proposed Laws authorized by a majority of the Members of the Parliament who voted against the Proposed Laws and desire to forward such arguments;

and

STATEMENT showing the alterations proposed to be made to the Constitution.

Official publication puts no inhibition on the robustness of the argument:

CONSTITUTION ALTERATION (DEMOCRATIC ELECTIONS)
1974
Argument against the proposed law
The Case for No
THIS IS A GIANT LABOR GERRYMANDER
DEMOCRACY COULD NOT SURVIVE UNDER THIS DECEITFUL PROPOSAL
IT WOULD MAKE A MOCKERY OF ONE VOTE-ONE VALUE

The proposed law also seeks to exercise over the States an authority which is outside the spirit of the Constitution—by dictating how their own elections should be carried out and thus altering the structure of some of the Parliaments.

The question on your ballot paper will deceitfully ask you to 'approve the proposed law for the alteration of the Constitution, entitled an Act to alter the Constitution so as to ensure that the Members of the House of Representatives and of the Parliaments of the States are chosen directly and democratically by the people'.

No Australian would disagree with such a sentiment, and in carefully choosing these deceitful words, the Government has deliberately and dishonestly hidden the controversial 'small print', the calculated deceptions, in the proposal.

IF YOU VOTE 'YES' YOU APPROVE A GIANT LABOR GERRYMANDER

There will be a fundamental change in your electoral laws—for the worse. We already have democratic elections. The proposal is to change the emphasis from **electors**—those old enough to vote—to people who are not electors. Buried in the proposed law (in Clauses the referendum question does not tell you about) is the provision that electorates should be made up of equal numbers of people.

Equal numbers of **electors**, which is what we have now, is democratic. Equal numbers of **people** regardless of whether they are voters is undemocratic.

If you vote 'yes' electorates would have to be changed, to include babes-in-arms and other children under 18, and un-naturalised migrants. A baby would not get a vote, but would have to be counted as a member of the electorate....

The passage I have quoted is about half the argument against the law. Such arguments are limited to 2,000 words. They compare in length with a British election address. Their intellectual content is invariably greater because they are confined to political issues, whereas an election address tells of the candidate's education, career and family. Each argument for and against a constitutional amendment is authorized by a majority of its supporters in both Houses.

The White Paper on the EEC referendum stated that there would be another White Paper explaining the Government's recommendation on how to vote. Every household would receive a popular version of this second White Paper and an explanation of how the referendum would be conducted. Influenced by the example of Australia, the Government proposed to send at the same time 'a single document containing a statement of between 1,000 and 2,000 words of each of the opposing views, together with answers given by each side to the same set of questions. This document would best be prepared by representatives of the main campaigning organisations representing the two points of view.'[8] In addition the Government proposed to establish for the period before the referendum an information unit to meet requests for relevant facts and interpretation of the renegotiated terms.

Although I believe the danger that the electors may be duped is exaggerated, I do believe it desirable that they should be better informed politically. We have seen that a referendum provides an incentive to educate the electors in its subject-matter. The general practice of holding referenda should also provide an incentive to the schools to give future electors some grounding in constitutional processes. We

86

could expect to have an electorate, not only better informed about current affairs, but at least familiar with such terms as 'Bill', 'amendment', 'repeal' and 'entrenched clause'. This is, I trust, a more persuasive argument than that the introduction of the constitutional referendum should be indefinitely postponed because of the electorate's present ignorance.

TIMING

An EEC fishing agreement signed just before the referendum is said to have resulted in Norway's No vote. If so, this was a matter of chance. But, with the opinion polls to guide it, might not a Government hold a snap referendum at the one point in time when it could secure a majority for its own point of view? The result of such a referendum could not be regarded as representative. Opinion polls are not reliable predictors of referendum results. None the less they are likely over the years, provided the same question is asked consistently, to reveal the trend of opinion. They tell a Government, not whether it will win a referendum, but what is the best or least bad time to hold it.

The danger is real if the Government is free to hold snap referenda. If referenda are held only on Bills that have been debated in Parliament, the Government can hardly have such nice control over their timing. Indeed the danger of a snap referendum is less than that of a snap election. Our first referendum, on EEC membership, had to be a plebiscite. But there was no scope for Machiavellian timing. The restrictions accepted by the Labour Party in its manifesto were at least as great as those on a constitutional referendum. The EEC referendum had to be held after the completion of the renegotiation and not later than 10 October 1975—that is to say, within a year of the general election.

VOTING ON PARTY LINES

As a general rule, it is undesirable for a Government to offer or threaten to resign if its recommendation is rejected in a referendum. Opponents of the Government who agree with its recommendation are then tempted to vote against it in order to get their own party into power. The point of the referendum may then be lost. Even without an attempt by the Government to make a referendum a vote of confidence, it is possible some electors may vote according to party allegiance if the issue is one on which Government and Opposition are divided. This would be most likely to occur during Britain's first few national referenda while referenda were still unfamiliar.

The danger is inherent in party politics and can be judged only against the alternative. Electors are at least more likely to vote on the merits of an issue when treating it singly. If there were a referendum on the electoral system, many Conservative and Labour supporters would vote for proportional representation. They would never vote for a Liberal candidate merely because he favoured proportional representation. We have seen evidence that a majority of the electorate would like the practice of holding referenda to be introduced. But when Mervyn Taggart stood at Reigate in February 1974 on a platform of real democracy, people's power and the referendum, he polled only 254 votes out of 60,003.

10
ALTERNATIVES TO THE REFERENDUM

CHURCHILL USED TO remind us that democracy was a dreadful system but that other systems were worse. If we believe in the referendum, it can only be for the same reason. We have just defended one of its aspects on the ground that it is less bad than a general election. We shall now consider in some detail four of the alternatives to the referendum. Two of these are already part of our political system: a free vote; a general election under the first-past-the-post electoral system. The other two would require changes: a general election under the single transferable vote (or proportional representation); special legislative procedures (though we already have a single entrenched clause).

SPECIAL LEGISLATIVE PROCEDURES

A written Constitution, national boundaries, national sovereignty, a fundamental Act, anything indeed thought important enough may be made subject to change only by some exceptional procedure. Such 'entrenched clauses' will usually but not always be a conservative influence. If joining the EEC had needed the support of 66⅔ per cent of MPs voting in the Commons (and if MPs had voted as in fact they did when only a simple majority was needed), Britain would not have joined—not at least on 1 January 1973. But, given that Denmark and the Republic of Ireland, two of Britain's traditional trading partners, were going to join the EEC, it was arguably more conservative to join with them than it would have been to become separated from them economically by staying out.

The main advantage of entrenched clauses has nothing to do with conservatism. It is that they tend to prevent change from being undertaken as the result of a transient majority. Hence they tend to prevent national dithering. Suppose that Britain had joined the EEC with the support of 66⅔ per cent of MPs voting. Thereafter it would have needed the support of 66⅔ per cent of MPs voting, or a swing of at least 33⅓ per cent, to take Britain out of the EEC.

A specified majority in the legislature is a favourite and generally effective means of entrenchment. The abundance of legislatures under a federal Constitution allows the variations on this principle which we have already mentioned. Article 5 of the United States Constitution reads:

The Congress, whenever two-thirds of both Houses shall deem it necessary, shall propose amendments to this Constitution, or, on the application of two-thirds of the several States, shall call a Convention for proposing amendments, which, in either case, shall be valid to all intents and purposes, as part of this Constitution, when ratified by the legislatures of three-fourths of the several States, or by conventions in three-fourths thereof ...

Another way of entrenching a clause is to require that its amendment (or repeal) must be passed by two successive legislatures. This requires a Government to obtain a mandate for it. If the subject is important enough, the intervening election may be largely fought on it. To require acceptance of an amendment in a referendum is a more precise form of entrenchment. In a referendum a specific majority of more than 50 per cent may be required. An alternative or additional requirement is the support of a specified proportion of the registered electors. The abolition of Scottish pubs requires the support of 55 per cent of those voting and of 35 per cent of the registered electors.

In practice a majority in a referendum will usually be required in addition to a majority in the legislature or in one chamber thereof. Only simple majorities may be required both in the referendum and in the legislature, or special conditions may be associated with both or either. A constitutional amendment in Denmark must be supported in the *Folketing* by a majority of those voting and also in a referendum both by a simple majority of those voting and by 40 per cent of the registered electors. Denmark has separate provisions for measures transferring national sovereignty to international federations. They become law automatically if supported by five-sixths of MPs (not merely of those voting). If supported by a simple majority of MPs voting, but not by five-sixths of all MPs, such a measure can be put to referendum and will become law unless rejected by a majority of those voting and 30 per cent of the registered electors. Under one provision it needs a virtually unanimous *Folketing* to concede national sovereignty. Under another a simple majority in the *Folketing* can concede it despite majority opposition of the electors in a referendum with a low turnout. The 141 out of 179 Danish MPs who voted for joining the EEC were not enough. The issue was determined by the referendum of October 1972, when 63.3 per cent voted for joining with a turnout of nearly 90 per cent.

Dicey looked to the referendum to entrench fundamental features of the British Constitution. That Home Rule could be passed by a transient majority in the Commons was not possible when he expressed fear of it, since any Bill could be vetoed by the Lords. It was, however, made true by the Parliament Act 1911. Since the Parliament Act 1949, all that stands between the Commons and most constitutional amendments is one year's delay by the Lords and the possible refusal of the Royal Assent. The Sovereign might withhold the Royal Assent from a Bill which overthrew British democracy, and might require a general election before granting it to a Bill which profoundly altered its character. But this safeguard, while valuable, is problematical.

The British Constitution does have its one entrenched clause: the lifetime of Parliament cannot be prolonged without the consent of the Lords. In principle other clauses could be entrenched by giving the Lords a veto over their amendment. In practice the Lords, being undemocratic in its composition, is frightened to use strong powers except when the purpose is manifestly democratic. The referendum is a better means of entrenchment than the Lords' veto or than a requirement for an exceptional majority in the Commons. We have seen that the United States Constitution was paternalist in intent. One unquestionable advantage of entrenchment by referendum is that constitutional amendments, if passed, are accepted by the people as right.

FREE VOTE

The rare free votes in the House of Commons are the vestige of Burkean representative government. MPs are expected to vote in them according to their consciences. Free votes are free of party dictation— free of the Whips. At worst they are a workable way of deciding cross-party issues. Since they are determined by party authorities, a particular vote may be free for some MPs and not others. If it were ever decreed by Statute that free votes should be held on certain Bills, it could still be the party authorities who determined whether they were truly free.

What influence can an elector hope to have on an issue, such as capital punishment, on which a free vote is traditional? During each election campaign he can ask candidates their views and take their answers into account in deciding how he votes. He is unlikely, however, to sacrifice his traditional party allegiance to cast his vote solely on capital punishment. All (or both) candidates standing in his constituency may in any case hold the same views on it. If his own party's candidate shares his view, he can vote for him with good heart, but without having any influence on capital punishment.

In theory the free vote allows the electorate virtually no influence. In practice the Commons does not like to pass laws that are far ahead of public opinion. Since their votes are public knowledge, the less principled MPs cannot be relied on to vote according to their consciences at all. It may be argued that, in so far as MPs are influenced by their constituents' opinions, referenda are less necessary. But an MP may be influenced in particular by vociferous constituents: he may think them more representative than they are; he may assume that the vociferous feel more strongly on the issue—that the non-vociferous are less likely to vote against him if offended on it. Another danger of the free vote is that an MP may be concerned to appease his constituency association rather than his constituents: the support of his constituents will be worth little if he is not renominated as his party's candidate.

Few MPs actually vote against their consciences on a free vote. But there is no doubt that, to avoid incurring unpopularity, many abstain from voting. This is easy since, by definition, the Whips are off. They need not abstain in a conscientious-looking manner. They can contrive not to be at Westminster for the division:

> Why, when the Labour party is supposed to be so strongly opposed to prescription charges, and when the [Conservative] Government is attempting to insist on imposing these charges for contraceptives, did the Government get its way in the Commons by the surprisingly large majority of 243 to 126 (just about four times its nominal majority), especially when many Tory MPs were known to be unhappy about the Government's decision? The explanation is simple: the Labour Party allowed its MPs a free vote. A large number of Labour MPs went home to bed; a few had no strong views on the subject; several of the Catholics wanted to keep out of the dispute, while other members told their colleagues they had no desire to get on the wrong side of the well-organised Catholic pressure groups in their constituencies.[1]

MPs are more likely to behave in this faint-hearted manner when they calculate that their votes cannot affect the result. At best, unless there is unofficial pairing or (which is improbable on a delicate issue) the abstainers are fortuitously balanced, the country gets a false impression of opinion in the House. At worst the abstainers miscalculate—easy when there are no Whips to count heads and ensure the requisite number of votes—and an unrepresentative decision is recorded. The free vote encourages the tradition of doing good by stealth while, for want of a secret ballot in the Commons, making it impossible of fulfilment.

Even if its failings be accepted, the free vote is adequate to deal only with those cross-party issues which the electors generally regard as subordinate to the party issues. Few electors would value a vote on capital punishment more than the right to choose between Labour, Conservative and Liberal. Many think that which party is in power is less important than whether we stay in the EEC. For many electors, therefore, denial of a vote on EEC membership would have amounted to disfranchisement. There are likely to be more important cross-party issues in future. Partly this is because the world is becoming more international and there will be more issues affecting national sovereignty.

Partly it is because, as Anthony Crosland first impressed on us, in an affluent society a variety of social issues may affect electors more than the conflict between capital and labour.

There remain two kinds of often overlapping cross-party issues on which a free vote is appropriate: that which (unlike EEC membership) genuinely depends on complex technical arguments; that in which the majority of electors are not greatly interested (whether because it affects only a minority or because it affects the majority but not significantly).

The free vote and the referendum do not exclude one another. Jeremy Thorpe demanded a free vote on whether there should be an EEC referendum and (if this should prove affirmative) a second free vote on whether the result should be binding or consultative.[2] It would be a useful convention that any vote in Parliament on whether a Bill should be put to referendum should be a free one.

A free vote might be allowed on a Bill in an attempt to avert a referendum. The Lords twice amended the National Health Service Reorganization Bill 1973 in favour of free contraception. Amending it a third time would have brought the Parliament Act 1949 into operation: the Bill would have been passed without the Lords' amendment after a year's delay. After a debate in which patronizing reference was made to reactionary views in another place, the Lords decided without a division not to insist on its amendment. It would surely have called for a referendum if it had had the power. Fearing this, the Conservative Government might have allowed its own supporters a free vote. If the Commons had supported the Government in a free vote, the Lords might conceivably have refrained from calling for a referendum. If the Commons had voted in favour of free contraception, that would have ended the matter.

GENERAL ELECTION

The general election of 1831 was fought on parliamentary reform, that of 1886 on Home Rule, that of December 1910 on the Lords' powers. In each case, since the dominant issue divided the parties, the electors had an uncomplicated opportunity to vote on it. Each of these general elections was held for the purpose of deciding a certain issue. Without the controversies over Reform, Home Rule and the Lords' powers, there would not have been elections in 1831, 1886 and December 1910. The 1831 election followed one in 1830; the 1886 election followed one in 1885; that in December 1910 was the second in a year and was decided on after a referendum had been considered as an alternative. If an election has to be held specifically to decide an issue, then, as Balfour argued in November 1910 in his main campaign speech to the London Conservatives in the Albert Hall, a referendum is less expensive and inconvenient.

Under our first-past-the-post electoral system, the result of a general election on a particular issue can be grossly inaccurate. The 1886 election was the one which best served the function of a referendum. Not only did Gladstone fight it specifically on Home Rule, but it was uncomplicated by split votes. The pro-Home-Rule candidates polled almost as many votes as the antis. When allowance is made for uncontested constituencies, it is evident there was a pro-Home-Rule majority in the country. Yet the election resulted in an anti-Home-Rule majority in the Commons of 104.

Let us assume hypothetically that all votes in an election are cast on one issue. Even when all the constituencies are contested, it does not follow that the total votes cast give an accurate measure of opinion: some electors in safe seats will not bother to vote. In a referendum every vote counts, and the electors know it.

In practice not all the votes in 1886 were cast on Home Rule. At most elections there is not even a single dominating issue. The parties are divided on several important issues and there is no sure way of estimating which has determined the most votes. The best guides, the opinion polls, have no constitutional force. A party winning 51 per cent of the seats (possibly on a minority of the popular vote) is entitled to pass legislation proposed in its manifesto even though the polls show 90 per cent of the electors opposed to it. Equally, if the Government passes legislation supported by 90 per cent of the electors, the Opposition party can repeal it when next in office provided it has mentioned its intention in its election manifesto. The use of referenda would make important legislation more permanent. The referendum might have saved the steel industry from some of its changes of status. If Britain's membership of the EEC had been endorsed in a referendum in 1972, it would have ceased to be an issue.

A commitment in a party's election manifesto is unlikely to be as precisely worded as in a referendum. It must also be said that, with their confidence in British notions of representative government, politicians are capable of ignoring even an unambiguous commitment. The Labour Party promised to hold a referendum (or an election) on the EEC in its manifestos for both the February and October 1974 elections. The October manifesto promised that the result would be binding on the Government. Yet there were MPs who opposed the EEC referendum after the October election (without suggesting that another election should be held instead on the completion of the renegotiation). They did so on the ground, not that circumstances had changed since the commitment was made, but simply that they did not believe electors should be involved in the processes of government. Burke himself would have condemned a party that made a promise before an election and blandly broke it afterwards.

There was never any reason to believe that the Labour Government would in fact renegue on its commitment. But it is a disturbing thought that it could have done so had it wished. A party knows that, if it dishonours an election pledge, its opponents can shame it before the electorate and make it lose votes. This is a deterrent. Being themselves opposed to the referendum, however, the Conservatives and Liberals would not have complained if the Labour Government had dishonoured its referendum pledge. They would probably have congratulated it on accepting their own superior judgement. Few in the contemporary British Parliament would have been concerned that the electors had been betrayed. A referendum has the advantage over an election that it can make a commitment not only precise but legally binding.

EEC membership reminds us again that important issues do not necessarily divide the parties. Bruce Campbell's advocacy of a referendum in 1969 was on the ground that, since all three parties favoured membership, an election afforded no opportunity to vote on it. Individual candidates opposed it of course, but this afforded a choice only to electors in certain constituencies. Virtually nowhere could electors vote for or against EEC membership while also exercising their traditional right to vote Conservative, Labour or Liberal. Labour subsequently changed its policy on the EEC, but it was never unequivocally opposed to membership. Few Conservative and Liberal anti-Marketeers will have entertained the idea of voting for the Labour Party because it opposed EEC membership on the existing terms. A general election afforded a satisfactory, if oblique, means of voting on the EEC only when Labour promised to hold a referendum. Since even then Enoch Powell and other Conservative sympathizers had to vote for a party to which they were strongly opposed, it would surely have been better to have constitutional provision for a referendum in the first place.

SINGLE TRANSFERABLE VOTE

We should remove some of the objections to a general election as an alternative to a referendum if we replaced our first-past-the-post electoral system with the single transferable vote (STV), popularly known as proportional representation or PR. One of its effects would be to prevent the kind of unrepresentative result that occurred in the 1886 election. If the STV had been in operation, there would probably have been a pro-Home-Rule majority in the Commons as in the country.

It is unfortunate that the STV is known as proportional representation. Its opponents are able to imply, even to believe, that its advocates want mathematical accuracy for its own sake, at the cost of sacrificing strong one-party to weak coalition government. The STV is based on constituencies with about six members, and electors vote for candidates in order of preference. This does not produce exact proportional representation, though it assures a party with the following of the

95

Liberals a substantial representation. This does not mean weak government. If there are only two parties capable of forming a Government—only two parties effectively to represent all the views in the country—both are going to be coalitions themselves. A formal Coalition Government which included the Centre could be more stable than the Government of a Left-wing or Right-wing party divided between moderates and extremists.

Be that as it may, the main advantage of the STV is that it removes the fear of 'splitting the vote'. The most serious party division in the Labour Party since the war was over unilateral disarmament. Because of our electoral system it proved impossible to resolve it at the polls. In 1954 Sir Richard Acland, the Labour MP for Gravesend, resigned his seat and recontested it (though the pending by-election was overtaken by a general election) against an official Labour candidate on the issue of the hydrogen bomb. The Labour vote was split and Gravesend duly won by the Conservative candidate. Under the STV, Sir Richard could have fought against the official Labour candidate without splitting the vote. Labour electors could have put the official candidate or Sir Richard as first choice with the other as second choice. Labour would definitely have won the seat. Whether the official candidate or Sir Richard had succeeded would have reflected fairly the views of Labour voters in Gravesend on unilateral disarmament. The STV has an evident advantage over the referendum in resolving issues which exercise one party in particular.

Issues cutting across parties can be resolved by the STV. It is the electoral system in the Republic of Ireland. In the Republic's 1922 general election it satisfactorily decided the issue of whether to accept the treaty offered by Britain. Electors were able to vote for their own parties and within them for pro-treaty and anti-treaty candidates (with the result a pro-treaty majority in the *Dáil*).

If the STV had been in operation in the United Kingdom in 1970, every constituency could have had pro-EEC and anti-EEC Conservative candidates and pro-EEC and anti-EEC Labour candidates. There could also have been pro-EEC Liberal candidates in every constituency. It is doubtful if there would have been enough anti-EEC Liberal candidates to go round.

Anti-EEC Conservative electors could have given their second preferences to pro-EEC Conservative candidates. Alternatively, Conservative electors who felt, like Enoch Powell, that keeping out of the EEC was the main issue could have given their preferences in order to anti-EEC Conservative candidates, anti-EEC Liberal candidates, and anti-EEC Labour candidates. The resulting Commons would probably have had either a Conservative majority or the makings of a Conservative-Liberal Coalition. It would almost certainly have had a pro-EEC majority cutting across the parties, with the anti-

EEC minority also cutting across the parties.

The precision of the issues voted on would have made it less likely that either individual MPs or parties would renegue on commitments. Each MP would have committed himself to vote for or against joining the EEC (unless of course he had told the electors he was undecided). Thereafter he might have claimed some discretion if the terms were different from those expected, but that would have been between him and his constituents. There would have been no question that his party could require him to change his views. Hence there could have been no serious dissension within the parties over the EEC, and Enoch Powell would not have needed to vote Labour. In preserving party unity the STV could have served as well as a referendum.

It could also have served as well as a referendum in giving electors a say in whether Britain should join the EEC and hence in inciting them to learn more about the issue. It would have had a slight advantage over a referendum in that electors could not have been tempted to conceal their true views on EEC membership in order to vote for or against the Government.

We have, however, been making a large assumption: that in 1970 there would have been enough pro-EEC and anti-EEC Conservative and Labour candidates to give all the electors a choice. It is doubtful if in 1970 EEC membership was sufficient of an issue to produce such an array of candidates. It may have become one later. But, if a general election must be held to resolve an issue, the advantage is with a referendum.

The STV could in principle have resolved many of the great issues of the last century: Home Rule; the Lords' powers; tariff reform; food taxes arising from Empire Free Trade; appeasement before the war; unilateral disarmament after it; EEC membership. But in nearly every case it would have meant a special election.

Suppose that in 1970 there had been a sufficient range of candidates to enable virtually all the electors to vote for or against EEC membership. Who would have financed and assisted all these candidates? At best, would not the official party candidates have had a significant financial and organizational advantage over the others? It would be difficult for the state to give financial assistance without encouraging frivolous candidatures.

There is many an issue on which it is desirable to let the electors pronounce but which will not induce hundreds of candidates to stand in a single election. This gives the referendum an obvious advantage. With the STV, on the other hand, progress can be made slowly. Moreover an impact can be made on Parliament by those outside. The referendum makes this possible only if accompanied by the initiative, whereby electors may introduce legislation.

In theory someone wishing to influence Parliament stands as a candidate himself. In practice the first-past-the-post electoral system makes it a waste of time to oppose the party candidates. Under the STV a Conservative supporter who feels insufficient is being done about pollution stands as a Conservative Anti-Pollutionist, preferably in a constituency where pollution is something of an issue. He undertakes to accept the Conservative whip on all matters except those relating to pollution. Since it is known he cannot split the vote, it is perfectly possible for him to be elected.

Enid Lakeman argues that a general election under the STV avoids the problems arising both from the wording of the question in a referendum and from the electors' lack of specialized knowledge. At the 1970 election the electors 'would have been able to leave the technicalities to their elected representatives, while at the same time ensuring that the general inclination of those representatives was for or against the European Community as the case may be'.[3] As against that, the electors would have voted on an imprecise issue. In 1970 this was largely inevitable because the exact terms on which Britain could join the EEC were unknown. All in all, the STV in 1970 would have been a poor substitute for a referendum on the European Communities Bill at the end of 1972.

In dealing with appeasement the STV would have had an advantage over the referendum. Enid Lakeman long ago pointed out that, if there had been an election between Munich and the outbreak of the Second World War, 'public opinion could not have been properly reflected by any system under which a vote cast for Churchill as a leading opponent of appeasement could have been counted as a vote for the party led by Chamberlain'.[4] Appeasement could never be a clear-cut issue. Nor is it practicable to hold a referendum on whether to declare war. Electors needed to be able to vote for anti-appeasement candidates, including Conservatives, who, if elected, could judge the Government's reactions to events as they occurred and oppose it when appropriate.

Fortunately the STV and the referendum are not strictly alternatives. The introduction of the STV would improve the conduct of politics in various ways. It would reduce but not obviate the need for referenda. One of Enid Lakeman's arguments in favour of the STV is its superior compatibility with the referendum.[5] It would make the Commons more representative of opinion in the country. Hence it would reduce the chance that Government legislation might be rejected in a referendum.

If the use of the STV enabled an election result to demonstrate clearly the electorate's opinion on an issue, a successful referendum on the relevant Bill when all its stages had been otherwise completed would be a reaffirmation of that opinion after a passage of time. Such evidence that opinion was not transient could compensate for a possible narrow majority in a referendum.

11
SUITABLE SUBJECTS

MANY DIFFERENT COUNTRIES hold referenda on constitutional amendments. One reason why the citizens of Massachusetts rejected the first Constitution offered to them in 1778 was that it had been drawn up, not by a Constituent Assembly, but by a normal legislature. Since the electors were being allowed the last word, this might seem pedantic. None the less the electors' instinct was sound. A Parliament is elected to carry on the business of government, not to change its basis.

A change in the basis of Government cannot necessarily be put right at the next election. This is the difference between raising income tax on the one hand and joining the EEC or abolishing the Monarchy on the other. There is now support on both Right and Left for introducing a Bill of Rights, which would protect civil liberties. Future Governments would persuade themselves that emergencies justified them in ignoring even a Bill of Rights unless it were in some way entrenched.

It is the delegation of national sovereignty which has made the referendum an issue in the United Kingdom. Douglas Jay argued in *The Times*[1] that membership of the EEC afforded a unique case for the referendum. *The Times* itself, opposing all referenda, argued fairly that membership of NATO had involved an even bigger international commitment. Britain would have been a better member of NATO if membership had been endorsed in a referendum. As it is, the British have tended to be unwilling supporters of NATO, thinking of it as American-imposed. All major international commitments should be put to referendum. While, as *The Times* argued, it would have been impossible to hold a referendum on the outbreak of the Second World War, it would have been both possible and appropriate to hold one on the alliance with Poland which contracted Britain to go to war.

The Interparliamentary Union congress at Berne in 1952 asked member countries to incorporate in their Constitutions provisions permitting the transfer of sovereignty to international federations. Denmark promptly included such provisions in its new Constitution in 1953. Twenty years later they were invoked to hold the referendum on joining the EEC. Such provisions must make for international co-operation and reduce domestic strife. In Britain the debate on joining the EEC got mixed up with the debate on whether there should be a referendum on joining.

Sovereignty can be delegated downwards as well as upwards. Jeremy Thorpe attacked the EEC referendum by raising the question of one on Scottish or Welsh devolution: 'Will the people as a whole, or the Scots, or the Welsh, be asked to give their "full-hearted consent" through a referendum? If not, why not?'[2] Both the United Kingdom electors as a whole and the Scottish and Welsh electors separately should indeed give their consent. The Scots and Welsh electors should also be asked to endorse their self-governing Constitutions. The Conservatives at least should approve: in 1911 they sought to amend the Parliament Bill to provide for a referendum on Irish, Scottish or Welsh Home Rule.

All else apart, MPs are not unbiassed judges of whether power should be delegated upwards to Brussels or downwards to Edinburgh or Cardiff. They have a vested interest in keeping it at Westminster. There is a case for holding referenda on all matters in which MPs have vested interests, in particular their finances. When in 1974 MPs were considering the small moral advance of a register in which their financial interests would be made public, a Harris poll conducted for *Midweek* (BBC Television) found that:

56 per cent of people believed that MPs should receive no salaries or fees other than their parliamentary salaries and expenses;

66 per cent believed no MP should hold a full-time job outside the Commons;

57 per cent believed MPs should not be directors of companies.

79 per cent believed MPs should not be sponsored by or paid an allowance by trade unions;

78 per cent (pending these reforms) favoured a compulsory register of MPs' interests.

There is no virtue in allowing MPs a free vote on feathering their own nests. The salaries and expenses they draw (with provision for increases with inflation) and the other financial interests which they are allowed should all be embodied in a Bill and put to referendum. The electors would assuredly be prepared to pay MPs well for their work as MPs provided they gave up other financial interests. Or, if MPs think there are good reasons why they should retain outside interests, let them explain them so that they may be judged by those with no vested interest to make their judgement suspect. Once established in a democratic manner, MPs' own powers and privileges should be entrenched.

The need for a referendum is perhaps greatest where electoral practices are involved. A gerrymandering Bill cannot fairly be voted on in retrospect at a general election in which the constituencies have been determined by it: any support the Government loses for manifest trickery may be more than offset by the technical gain.

Switzerland introduced in 1919 a system of proportional representation for elections to the National Council.

By ensuring that parties were represented according to their relative strength, the system meant the end of Radical dominance in the federal government and enabled minority groups to make their voices better heard in the affairs of the nation.[3]

Because of Radical dominance, it is unlikely that the Swiss electoral system would have been reformed without a referendum. In Britain, so long as we eschew the referendum, it will be difficult to persuade either the Labour or Conservative Party to reform the electoral system that encourages the 'two-party system' from which they have both benefited.

Although the Constitution of the French Fourth Republic gave the Prime Minister a right of dissolution when two Governments had been defeated by absolute majorities within eighteen months, tradition deterred its invocation. Finally Edgar Faure invoked it in 1955 when he had been refused a vote of confidence effectively over whether there should be an early election. Holding an election to decide whether there should be an election was manifest nonsense. It brought the Prime Minister's power to recommend a dissolution, and the Fourth Republic itself, into disrepute. The Constitution of the Fourth Republic allowed referenda only on constitutional amendments. Had it allowed one on whether to hold an election, the Fourth Republic might not subsequently have collapsed.

There is a case for holding a referendum on any important Government decision that has something of an irrevocable nature. Few decisions are physically irrevocable, but many involve so much capital investment and reorganization that there must be great resistance to rescinding them. Nationalization of a major industry and the choice of a new capital city are examples. During our lifetimes it is likely that energy crises, population crises and the like will require the country to take decisions of a different order from those customarily left to Governments. These decisions will have such an effect on the traditional way of life that it will be impossible to impose them on a people no longer conditioned to obey authority unquestioningly. They will need to be taken by the people themselves. It is desirable that the people should acquire practice in decision-making when less important issues are at stake.

Introducing his Bill under the ten-minute rule in 1967, Harold Gurden visualized that referenda would be held on subjects that 'create wide public concern and about which the political parties, or, in the main, Members of Parliament, have never sought a mandate from the public, and [on] which in General Elections the public have had no opportunity at all to express their view'.[4] Two examples he gave were the legalization of brothels (an issue at the time in Birmingham) and blood sports. We are concerned now with ordinary Bills that have no quality of constitutional amendment nor anything irrevocable about them. Those suitable to be put to referendum are likely to be either Private Members' Bills or Government Bills of a kind on which a free vote is traditionally allowed. On a cross-party issue such as EEC membership, which is likely to be regarded as more important than the party issues, a referendum is essential if electors are not to be effectively disfranchised. Such issues are rare. There are many more on which referenda are desirable. Notable among them are Bills on subjects affecting people's everyday lives, because the electors will both be well informed and feel committed to whatever decision is taken.

Immigration, industrial relations and incomes policies all come in this category. Often of course the electors know more about their own needs and wishes than MPs. This is true of simple subjects like putting the clock back and more substantial ones like education. The United States Congress is at least legislating for its own children. In Britain the many MPs, including Labour ones, who send their own children to public schools are legislating for other people's children. Buckinghamshire County Council held referenda on comprehensive schools. There should be national referenda on major Education Bills dealing with such issues as comprehensive schools and the school-leaving age.

Any Bill affecting civil liberties should be put to referendum. Often there is a conflict between the interests of the state and the citizen. The question relevant to referenda is whether the citizen can see the state's interest better than the legislator can see the citizen's. Where civil liberties are at stake, the citizen is the better judge because Ministers and MPs rarely suffer the same lack of consideration at the hands of the police and the bureaucracy as do ordinary citizens.

Neither the Road Safety Act 1967 nor the Dangerous Drugs Act 1967 would have been passed in its existing form if it had needed a majority in a referendum. Under the Road Safety Act the police may impose a breath test on a teetotal driver whose rear light fails as he is driving along or who is run into by another motorist. They may also impose a breath test on a driver who they think has had a drink even though he is manifestly sober and they have no reason to think he has drunk more than the law allows. Under the Dangerous Drugs Act a respectable English teacher and her son have been searched in the street without any ground for suspicion; Lady Diana Cooper's house has been raided by police on the strength of an anonymous telephone call; and a meeting of the Young Communist League has been broken up without the discovery of any drugs. These two Acts made Britain, by strict definition, a police state. Even in a free country the police subject a citizen to intimate investigation when they have reason to suspect he may have broken the law. The distinctive characteristic of a police state is that this happens without grounds for suspicion.

Let us examine the Road Safety Act 1967 further and consider how it might have differed had it been subject to a referendum. A drunk driver is now convicted of the same crime as a sober one with a blood-alcohol level a little above the limit of 80 milligrammes per 100 millilitres, which is a technical offence comparable to driving at 35 m.p.h. in a restricted area. No doubt the Act was intended to tar technical offenders with the same brush as the drunks. In practice it has whitewashed the drunks. Many drivers boast of convictions under the Road Safety Act since, whether or not it is true, they can say they were sober. Few boasted of the old drunk-driving convictions. If the intention of the Act was to save lives, why does the Government not have breathalysers on sale in pubs, garages and police stations? Not to do so is the equivalent of imposing a 30 m.p.h. speed limit and forbidding the use of speedometers. The Act is a means less of emptying the hospitals than of filling the prisons.

What kind of Bill would have been necessary to gain a majority in a referendum? The police would have been empowered only to impose a breath test if they had reason to believe a driver was under the influence of drink. (The original motive for introducing the breathalyser was the convincing police claim that they often knew a driver was drunk but could do nothing to prove it.) If a general blood-alcohol limit of 80 mg/100 ml was to be imposed, there would have had to be provision for a driver to take a Government test (for a fee) to show that he was competent to drive with a higher blood-alcohol level. A driver who passed would have been given a certificate showing his own personal permitted blood-alcohol limit. This would have meant people need not refrain from drinking or driving unnecessarily. More important, it would have called the bluff of all the drunken drivers who now persuade themselves and their friends that they are safe. Lastly, the Act would have needed to contain assurances about the provision of public transport. When Barbara Castle, the Minister of Transport responsible for the Road Safety Act, was asked what she expected people to do at Christmas, she mentioned the sharing of cars (with one driver reconciling himself to abstemiousness) and the use of taxis. Marie Antoinette at least had the excuse that she was not a twentieth-century Socialist Minister.

It has to be explained how the Road Safety Act 1967 could be passed even under the present political system. It empowers police to impose a breath test on a driver if they 'suspect him of having alcohol in the body'.[5] This misuse of language led drivers to believe they would be liable for breath tests only if they were suspected of having broken the law. One cannot 'suspect' someone of doing something innocent—of singing, dancing, talking, or drinking only as much as the law allows. MPs were not entirely deceived and showed signs of producing one of their rare rebellions. To get the Bill passed, Barbara Castle promised that the police would not wait for drivers outside pubs. It was left to her successor, Richard Marsh, to break her promise by permitting them to do so.

Misleading statements by British Governments or Government organs are all too common. For years the public was given to believe that there was a great rise in road accidents on Bank Holidays. In fact Bank Holiday accidents were in proportion to week-day ones. Since more drivers were taking unfamiliar routes on Bank Holidays, the standard of driving must have been higher. The anti-smoking propaganda in children's comics would show a named footballer suffering from loss of wind and attributing it to smoking. If asked, the footballer would admit he had never had any such experience. It is significant that all these admittedly extreme examples of misleading the public were inspired by puritanism. Drinking, Bank Holidays and smoking are all associated with enjoyment. The do-gooder needs no instruction in the doctrine that the end justifies the means, and our system of government gives him scope. It corrupts the legislators no less than it deprives the legislatees. A few referenda would improve the characters of both.

The connivance of the press at the suppression and misrepresentation of truth is itself a result of our system of government. Neither Parliament nor press feels able to force the Government to disclose information. Press correspondents are dependent on the goodwill of the Government, and in particular on the right to attend the press conferences of Government Departments. These conferences can be used to silence correspondents as much as inform them. Once the entire British press has been told something in confidence, there is no way it can be published. Russia at least has an underground press.

Parliament and press will never perform their proper function until they can force the Government to disclose information. Britain badly needs an equivalent of the American Freedom of Information Act, which, in the words of an envious British journalist, 'was perhaps even a seminal move in changing the role of American Government from one of absolute master towards one of almost biddable servant'.[6] We shall consider in Chapter 12 how we might get such an Act passed.

Money Bills should be excluded from those which can be put to referenda, just as they are from those which the Lords may delay for a year. The delay in holding referenda on Money Bills would be administratively inconvenient. Swiss experience shows that electors may not vote the taxes necessary to finance all the activities they wish the state to undertake. MPs might not do so without the party discipline that has superseded representative government. Governments themselves are disposed to raise less in taxes than is needed to control inflation, but at least the Treasury can bully them as it could not the entire electorate.

Certain subjects can never be suitable for holding referenda on because they are not suitable for passing laws about in the first place. Since 'The only freedom which deserves the name is that of pursuing our own good in our own way, so long as we do not attempt to deprive others of theirs',[7] unsuitable subjects include the opening of pubs and the Sunday opening of cinemas. No one has the right to stop others going to pubs or cinemas. Any necessary regulation of their opening and conduct can be achieved by licensing. Why then have Prohibition and local option on the opening of pubs accounted for a large proportion of the world's referenda? The explanation is fear of the temperance movement. While the cravenness of Governments and legislators is to be deplored, referenda at least provide an escape from it. If MPs are frightened to vote against the wishes of the temperance movement or the Catholic Church or the Lord's Day Observance Society or any other pressure group, let them delegate the work to us, the electors, who have less to lose.

REFERENDA AND MANDATES

The Canadian referendum of 1942 was held by the Liberal Government to obtain release from a specific anti-conscription pledge that the party had given at an election two years earlier. Either a referendum or a general election should be held on any important Bill for which the Government has no mandate, and more particularly on a Bill which offends against its mandate. Enoch Powell was right to condemn Edward Heath for remaining in office after adopting a statutory incomes policy such as he had condemned before he was elected. The present Labour Government got itself elected by promising not to introduce a statutory incomes policy. It should not need saying that it would now be wrong for it to do so without first holding either a referendum or an election.

How do Governments persuade themselves that it is in the country's interests for them to break promises to the electorate? The main argument is that a general election is disruptive. Fortunately a referendum is far less disruptive. It does not require the dissolution of Parliament. It does not mean that the work done on current Bills is lost. If a Government were defeated in a referendum on a Bill which offended against its mandate yet which it now thought essential to its policy, then of course it would have to resign and hold an election. If the Labour Government should find itself unable to rule without a statutory incomes policy, yet unable to gain a majority for it in a referendum, it would not be entitled to remain in office. Provision for referenda in these circumstances would deter parties from making cynical promises in the first place.

Further use might ultimately be made of the referendum as an alternative to an election. The Parliament Act 1911 reduced the maximum lifetime of Parliament from seven years to five. This was regrettable. Short Parliaments are for static societies. The transition of our own society from static to dynamic was completed during the Second World War. The limitation of five-year Parliaments was illustrated immediately afterwards by the groundnuts scheme. This was rushed, disastrously, in an attempt to get results with which to impress the electorate. Other long-term projects and responsibilities have simply been neglected. Governments have been reluctant to build the New Cities we need. One reason the energy and pollution crises caught us unawares was that they developed in a context a good deal longer than five years.

If the maximum lifetime of Parliament were restored to seven years, or, better, increased to ten or fifteen, there would be a greater danger of the Government's losing touch with the electorate. To offset this, the Sovereign might assume the discretion to dissolve Parliament (without or against the advice of the Prime Minister) when the Government appeared to have lost the confidence of the electorate beyond redemption, and greater use could be made of referenda. In these circumstances referenda would be more likely to be treated as votes of confidence in the Government: the Sovereign could hardly fail to consider the results of referenda on a number of Government Bills in deciding whether to dissolve Parliament. At least referenda are better substitutes for general elections than general elections for referenda.

12
WHO DECIDES ON A
REFERENDUM?

SOME OF THE ideas in the last chapter may have seemed alarmingly radical. I do not propose, however, that the electors should be able to requisition a referendum as in Switzerland. I propose that referenda should be held automatically on certain entrenched clauses, which is conservative, and that they should be held on other Bills only at the behest of some section of Parliament. Since Parliament would decide on the entrenched clauses in the first place, it would ultimately determine whenever a referendum was held. This is less than the overthrow of representative government.

Likely candidates for entrenchment are the Monarchy (but not, with talk of Disestablishment, the Protestant Succession), the electoral system, the lifetime of Parliament, the Lords' powers, national sovereignty, a Bill of Rights if we have one, and the Referendum Act providing for referenda.

Amendment (or repeal) of an entrenched clause should require the support of a third of the electors. The intention is to make change difficult. A Bill must state if its provisions are to be treated as entrenched. In a referendum on an ordinary Bill the result should be valid only if the votes on the winning side constitute a third of the electorate. If invalid, Parliament should proceed as though the referendum had not been held. An ordinary Bill endorsed in a referendum should not be capable of amendment without a further referendum. If the result of a further referendum is invalid, however, Parliament should again be free to act as it wishes. Ordinary Bills endorsed in referenda should not be entrenched like the Monarchy and national sovereignty. Otherwise Parliament could find it impossible to pass ordinary legislation merely because the electorate had lost interest in its subject-matter.

While some proportion other than a third may be chosen, it is important not to deviate from the principles. In Italy an ordinary Bill put to referendum becomes law if it is approved by a majority of those voting and if a majority of electors vote. Opponents of a Bill may therefore have a better chance of preventing it from becoming law by abstaining from voting: if a third of the electors support a

Bill and more than a sixth oppose it, it will become law; if a third support it and not more than a sixth oppose it, it will not become law. Incentives not to vote should always be avoided.

It may be disputed whether a Bill involves a change in an entrenched clause or in an ordinary Act previously endorsed in a referendum. To allow a judicial court to determine such disputes, as in the United States, would indeed be alien to the British Constitution. Nor is it necessary, since the Swiss Parliament recognizes constitutional amendments for itself. The responsibility should be given to the House of Lords, when it would be possible to exploit one of the anomalies of the British Constitution: that the House of Lords is both the upper chamber of the legislature and the highest court of the judiciary. As a law court the House of Lords usually sits, not in the legislative chamber, but in a committee room. The only members of the House who sit are the ten Lords of Appeal in Ordinary, the country's top judges who hold life peerages, and sometimes other peers who have held high judicial office. Convention (not law) excludes the lay peers when the House of Lords sits as a court. The Law Lords do sit and speak in the legislative House of Lords. In a debate which turned on a judicial interpretation of legislation the lay peers could be expected to leave the voting to the Law Lords or to accept their guidance. The lay peers would, however, decide for themselves whether the dispute could be regarded as solely judicial.

There would have to be provision in an emergency for Parliament alone to pass amending legislation normally requiring a referendum. This, like the prolongation of the lifetime of Parliament, could be made the subject of an absolute power of veto by the House of Lords.

The referendum does not afford so strong a means of entrenchment as a provision that an Act can be amended only by 66⅔ per cent of MPs or even of MPs voting. The intention is not to make change difficult for its own sake. Entrenchment by referendum will ensure that decisions are taken by the right people for the right reasons. It will prevent a major constitutional change from being effected by a majority of forty or fewer whipped MPs who are personally opposed to it. The mere provision of a special procedure for making constitutional changes will prevent future disputes about them.

To make constitutional changes subject to referendum is essentially to use the electors for the benefit of the Constitution. The electors gain most benefit from referenda when they are held on ordinary Bills. In 1911 the House of Lords was empowered to delay ordinary Bills (excluding Money Bills) for two years (since reduced to one), when instead it might have been empowered to put them to referendum. This decision not only deprived the electors of potential power. It weakened the Lords far more than was expected.

In principle the Lords now rejects a questionable Bill in order to provide time and stimulus for critical reflection. The Commons can pass it in a year's time if resolved to. In practice the Lords is reluctant to use even this limited delaying power. Since the traumatic experience of 1911, it has been on the defensive, conscious of itself as undemocratic, frightened of being abolished if it does not remain docile. This fear was reinforced when it objected to the post-war Labour Government's plan to nationalize the steel industry and had its delaying power reduced from two years to one for its presumption. The Lords is no longer Mr Balfour's poodle, but nor is it yet the watchdog of the people. Even with so popular a cause as free contraception, it could not keep its nerve, but heeded the advice of Lord Somers:

> This House, as one of the two Houses of Parliament, has been once or twice during the past few years in a rather precarious position. It is rather more secure now than it was a few years ago; but I think that it would be very unwise indeed for us deliberately to try to go against the other place in their decision. I think that a very likely outcome of that would be that we should no longer be given no [sic] powers of major legislation. Therefore, I think that it is purely worldly wisdom to abstain from this Amendment that we have been discussing.[1]

The Lords has been readiest to reject a Bill when it could feel, like George V requiring a second general election on the Parliament Bill, that it was upholding democracy. It opposed the Labour Government's boundary proposals in 1969 because they amounted to gerrymandering. The Lords would never need to feel inhibited about putting a Bill to referendum, which would be upholding democracy by definition. A referendum would induce more critical examination of a Bill than a mere delay in passing it.

The kinds of Bill which should be put to referendum cannot be defined satisfactorily in advance. This illustrates the weakness of written Constitutions. The novel issues of the future which would not be covered by a definition drawn up now could well be the ones on which referenda were most appropriate. A Government might in any case succeed in drafting a Bill to circumvent a statutory requirement for a referendum. In addition, the reason for putting a Bill to referendum might not be its subject-matter as such but the fact that the Government had no mandate for it. The only time the Lords need give a reason for putting a Bill to referendum is when it actually offends against the Government's mandate. This would be to create a presumption that the Government should resign if defeated in the referendum.

In the Republic of Ireland a majority of the members of the

Senate and not less than a third of the members of the *Dáil* may jointly petition the President to decline to sign and promulgate any Bill on the grounds that it 'contains a proposal of such national importance that the will of the people thereon ought to be ascertained'.[2] If the President is persuaded, he must not sign the Bill until it has been approved by the people in a referendum or reaffirmed by the *Dáil* after a general election. The Lords should not, as John St Loe Strachey envisaged, put to referendum only Bills to which it takes exception, but also those, like the European Communities Bill, 'of such national importance that the will of the people thereon ought to be ascertained'. Here again the influence of the Law Lords should be beneficial.

It need hardly be said that the self-confidence and judgement of the Lords would be helped by reforming its membership to exclude many of the hereditary peers, remove or reduce its conservative bias, and increase the representation of those outside professional politics. The Labour Party has opposed reform precisely because it would increase the Lords' influence.

Balfour of Burleigh's Reference to the People Bill 1911 proposed that, when the Lords rejected a Bill, either the Lords or the Commons should be able to put it to referendum. The Commons could be given this power despite the fact that it can now override the Lords after a year's delay. If the electorate supported a Bill, the Commons should be able to pass it forthwith. If the electorate rejected it, the Commons should not be free to proceed with it until a later Parliament, and then only subject to another referendum.

What would happen when a referendum was invalid because the votes on the winning side were less than a third of the electorate? If it had been held on the initiative of the Lords, the Commons should have the right to pass the Bill immediately. This is to say that the Lords should be able to invoke either its delaying power or its power to put a Bill to referendum, but not both. If, however, the referendum had been held on the initiative of the Commons, the Lords' delaying power should still operate. Otherwise, if the Lords rejected a recondite Bill for good reasons, the Commons might put it to referendum relying on the apathy of the electorate to enable it to override the Lords' delaying power.

In putting a Bill to referendum, the Lords would give up its right to invoke its delaying power. It would not put a Bill to referendum frivolously, for, if the electorate supported it, it would be passed more than a year earlier. It would put to referendum only Bills it approved of but thought the electorate should pronounce on (such as the European Communities Bill) and Bills it disapproved of and could reasonably hope the electorate might reject. The Lords would lose dignity if it criticized a Bill and put it to referendum only for it to receive overwhelming popular support—as did the Heath Government when the railwaymen supported their trade-union leaders by six to one in the compulsory ballot held under the Industrial Relations Act 1971. Even less would the Commons put a Bill to referendum frivolously: if the electorate supported it, it would be passed only a year or less earlier; whereas, if the electorate rejected it, it could not be passed during the current Parliament.

At present the knowledge that the Government can invoke the Parliament Act deters the Lords from proceeding with amendments. Similarly the Government's knowledge that the Lords could enforce a referendum would often persuade it to accept amendments—in the Commons no less than the Lords. The referendum, like the Parliament Act, could have a greater influence through its potential than its actual use. This would not be entirely a boon. Where the Government acted to avoid a referendum, it might be deferring to the uneducated, opinion-poll-recorded views of the electorate. It might, in short, misjudge what the result of a referendum would be. Experience of referenda should reduce this danger.

The most important use of the referendum is arguably to prevent electoral malpractice such as gerrymandering. Yet the Government may on occasion be able to gerrymander simply by refraining from implementing proposals of the Boundary Commission. There is then no Bill for the Lords to put to referendum. This eventually could be dealt with only by giving the Lords the power to put to referendum a Bill of its own rejected by the Commons. This would be a more radical measure and might be introduced after the country had gained experience of periodical referenda.

Balfour of Burleigh's Bill had one more proposal: that 200 MPs (out of a total of 670 at the time) could put to referendum a Bill passed by both the Commons and Lords. Roy Jenkins, in his role of the historian of the Parliament Bill, was scarcely less appalled by this proposal than some of the peers who condemned it in 1911: 'This was a wildly far-reaching proposal which would have made impossible any continuity of Government policy.'[3] It might have been in isolation. It would not be in conjunction with the provision that the result of a referendum should be invalid and be ignored unless the votes on the winning side were a third of the total electorate. Danish experience has demonstrated this. A third of Danish MPs can put a Bill to referendum, but it becomes law unless rejected both by a simple majority of those voting and by 30 per cent of the electorate. Two hundred MPs—or let us say a third of MPs—could not get a third of the British electors to the polls often enough to destroy all continuity in Government policy. The possibility of getting them to the polls from time to time would, however, make the Government treat Parliament seriously.

111

Knowledge that a Bill could be put to referendum, not merely by the Lords, but by the Opposition or by backbenchers in the Commons would make the Government far readier to accept amendments. Parliament might even work as it is supposed to. Far from detracting from representative government, the referendum would tend to restore it. In doing so, it would compensate for the present electoral system which, by discriminating against Centre parties, gives a choice between two parties whose manifestos will include extreme measures. With a docile Parliament, such a measure may become law as a concession to party militants though wanted by a majority neither of MPs nor of electors. Such amendments as are made are usually to mollify extraparliamentary pressure groups such as the CBI and the trade unions.

The failure of Governments to treat Parliament seriously has not merely had a dispiriting effect on MPs. It has driven good men out of politics and deterred others from entering. Ultimately this must reduce, if it has not already reduced, the calibre of Governments themselves. Nor are the ill-effects confined to politicians:

> Parliament's relative powerlessness in the policy formulating and administrative processes expresses itself in an essentially negative carping criticism of, and *ex post facto* investigation of, the departmental decisions it has been excluded from participating in. So Parliament's relationship with government departments is an essentially unfruitful one. MPs by their negative criticism and search for information add greatly to the burdens of civil servants and thus impede efficiency without being able to exercise any positive democratic control.[4]

The problem has long been acknowledged even among defenders of parliamentary orthodoxy. Various experiments have sought to make Parliament more powerful. For example, there have been changes in the committee system to try to introduce the qualities of the American Congressional Committees. The strength of the Congressional Committees derives, however, not from their procedures but from the separation of powers. Congress is independent. The President cannot dissolve it and put its members out of work when it defeats one of his measures. Having tried other ways of making the British Parliament more powerful, it is perhaps time to try giving it power.

There would be no logic in letting a third of MPs put to referendum a Bill passed by the Lords but not one rejected by the Lords. What is required is provision that an ordinary Bill passed by the Commons can be put to referendum either by a majority in the Lords or by a third of MPs. A Government would not need to resign if defeated in a referendum unless it had chosen to announce in advance that it would treat it as a vote of confidence or unless the reason for holding it was that the Lords had rejected a Bill as contrary to its mandate.

None of these proposals gives either Parliament or people any initiative in legislation. They all confine the referendum to use as a veto. The Swiss system has a more profound influence on Government:

> The Council is thus exposed to a cross-fire which is calculated to keep it from going to sleep. If the Council propose bad laws (if they are guilty of sins of commission) these laws will be rejected by the popular vote, or Referendum. If the Council do not wish to propose good laws (if they are guilty of sins of omission) the Popular Initiative steps in, making its own proposals.[5]

Even though there must be reservation about the initiative, the principle is sound. A compromise would be to give a third of MPs the right to put to referendum a Bill of their own, which should become law if supported by a third of the electors and a majority of those voting. This would be a way of correcting sins of omission. It would mean that the referendum was not just a veto but could be used constructively. It would quickly secure the passage of a British equivalent of the Freedom of Information Act.

This again is a more radical provision and should be introduced only after experience of referenda has been gained. Though Switzerland shows that referenda encourages responsibility and liberalism in electors, there are dangers during a transition period. It is one thing to have been drinking all one's life, another to start suddenly in middle age. If such radical provision were introduced overnight, Parliament and people might use it to restore capital punishment rather than to enhance the authority of the United Nations.

There is little danger that such provision will be introduced overnight. The question is how it will ever be introduced when the political parties have a vested interest in preserving the powers of Governments. The answer is that they are also anxious to win elections. Suppose first that referenda are held often enough to gain popularity. Thereafter whichever of the main parties looked like losing the next election would be tempted to promise an extension of the referendum.

BINDING OR CONSULTATIVE?

Cyril Smith, the Liberal MP, disagrees with his party's opposition to referenda. He wants many more held, but only, it seems, if they are consultative. He thinks an MP should be a representative, not a delegate, but an informed and humble representative:

> MPs should be aware of, and take account of, the views of the

113

people they represent—and if—over a reasonable wide field, they are no longer able to represent conscientiously those views—they should resign their seats![6]

This is excellent advice to MPs, but there is no way of enforcing it. There is no way of making MPs resign. It is not even clear from Cyril Smith's advice when they ought to. If referenda are made binding, an MP will always be free to resign when offended by the results.

Cyril Smith would like to give each MP the right to ask for referenda 'in his own constituency, say twice a year, on issues that he wished to test his constituents about'.[7] While the intention is admirable, it is difficult to believe such referenda would be much better than opinion polls. It is possible to conduct an effective national campaign on an important national issue, or an effective local campaign on an important local issue, but not an effective local campaign on a not particularly important national issue. Electors' views would not be informed and their replies might be influenced by the phrasing of the question.

Knowing referenda are consultative, electors may not be bothered to vote in them (in which respect they are less reliable than opinion polls). A bigger objection is the scope they afford for quarrelling after the event, which was spectacularly illustrated in the Belgian referendum of March 1950.

There was a lot of animosity towards Leopold III, who had taken the decision for Belgium to capitulate in the Second World War, and who was living in Switzerland. A consultative plebiscite asked: '*Êtes-vous d'avis que le Roi Leopold III reprenne l'exercice de ses pouvoirs constitutionels?*'[8] The consultative nature of the referendum was compounded by the ambiguity of the question. Leopold said that if he received less than 55 per cent support he would not resume the exercise of his prerogatives—but he did not say that he would abdicate. The Socialists maintained that only 66-70 per cent support, with at least a bare majority in each of Flanders, Wallonia and Brussels, would justify his return.

In the event he received 57.68 per cent support in the country as a whole, but 57.8 per cent in Wallonia and 51.8 per cent in Brussels voted against him. Since it had not been decided in advance what should happen in such circumstances, both sides claimed victory and the administration of government almost stopped. Elections in June gave the Catholic party, which supported Leopold, only 47.68 per cent of the votes but 108 out of 212 seats in the Chamber, the first parliamentary majority since 1914. After riots verging on civil war, Leopold reluctantly abdicated in favour of his son, Baudouin, in August.

It may be acceptable for a Government to ask for permissive powers in a referendum. The wartime Canadian Liberal Government was pledged not to send conscripted men overseas. In a plebiscite in 1942 it obtained release from this pledge. That no conscripted men were sent overseas does not mean the Government rejected the electors' advice. The plebiscite was consultative, but it would have made no difference if it had been binding.

The Labour Party's manifesto for the October 1974 election declared that the EEC referendum would 'be binding on the Government'. Like the Norwegian Labour Party before it, it promised to treat as binding a referendum which constitutionally would be only consultative. This could mean only that it would put the Whips on to enforce the result of the referendum. That the EEC was an issue on which Labour MPs had shown themselves ready to defy the Whip should not have mattered. Each Labour candidate was morally bound by the commitment in the manifesto unless he publicly dissociated himself from it before the election. Unfortunately the *folie des grandeurs* at Westminster means MPs cannot be relied on to keep promises to constituents. The Labour Leadership should have asked Labour candidates for specific assurances that they would honour the referendum pledge. Support from Conservative and Liberal MPs would always have enabled the Government to enforce a decision to remain in the EEC. It was uncertain whether it could enforce a decision to withdraw.

REFERENDUM COMMISSION

Once the decision is taken to make the referendum a permanent feature of the Constitution, an independent Referendum Commission should be established. Like the Boundary Commission, it would have a double role as consultant and arbiter. It would provide advice at once specialized and impartial. It would be responsible for disbursing financial assistance to campaigning organizations; sending pamphlets containing information and publicity (for and against) with polling cards; advising on the timing of referenda and the phrasing of the questions. Its functions would be even more important in local than in national referenda. Electors would be more dependent on official pamphlets for information about local than national issues. In local referenda too there will always be discretion in the phrasing of the question.

The phrasing of questions in national referenda on Bills debated in Parliament would be pre-ordained except that the Commission would need to watch for tendentiousness in their titles. A difficulty arises when what is at issue is not the principle of a Bill but a specific provision. Suppose the Lords had put the National Health Service Reorganisation Bill 1973 to referendum. The issue would have been the Government's failure to provide for free contraception. To vote for free contraception the electors would have had to reject the entire

Bill. The Bill could have been re-introduced with provision for free contraception, but there would have had to be a second referendum on it—because no one would have known for sure why the electors had rejected it initially. Putting an amendment to a Bill to referendum would be possible, but a more satisfactory solution might be a separate Bill which, if passed, would have the effect of modifying the operation of the first.

The Lords could have passed the National Health Service Reorganisation Bill on the understanding that the Commons would introduce a National Health Service Reorganisation (Free Contraception) Bill for it to put to referendum. Or, if the Lords had been given the power to put to referendum a Bill of its own rejected by the Commons, it would have been enough for it to introduce its own National Health Service (Free Contraception) Bill. When Commons and Lords (or Government and Opposition, or Government and backbenchers) disagreed on the best way of drafting Bills so that an issue might be put to referendum, the Commission could arbitrate. Without an arbiter, the Government might be tempted to include an unpopular meaure in a popular but barely relevant Bill.

Again like the Boundary Commission, the Referendum Commission would have no power. In local referenda the Department of the Environment could be expected to enforce its recommendations. In national referenda the Referendum Commission would rely, like the Boundary Commission, on its prestige and on the readiness of the Opposition to expose the Government as fraudulent if it ignored its recommendations. The Referendum Commission would have an advantage over the Boundary Commission. Given sensible entrenched rules for their conduct, referenda cannot be influenced by gerrymandering. Chicanery does not offer a Government a technical gain to offset the votes it will lose for condemnation by a respected arbiter.

13
WHAT WILL REFERENDA ACHIEVE?

SIR KEITH JOSEPH is right: we have a crisis of discipline brought about by permissiveness. But it does not follow that we should restore the old authoritarianism. The Russians also have a crisis of discipline brought about by permissiveness—by the political liberalization that followed Stalin's death. They recall that under Stalin discipline was good. Should they not restore Stalinist methods?

We know that the solution is for Russia to introduce democracy. Authoritarian discipline has broken down. It should be replaced by a new collective discipline—by government by consent. Broadly speaking, people obey rules for one of two reasons: because they are frightened of the consequences of disobedience; or because they accept the authority by which the rules have been formulated. In the twentieth century only democratic authority is acceptable.

There is industrial permissiveness in that the trade unions have power without responsibility. Edward Heath tried to solve this problem by taking power away from them—which was impossible even had it been desirable. The solution is to foist responsibility upon them. We, the victors in the Second World War, gave the German trade unions seats on the Boards of all important industries. Instead of complaining that the Germans work harder, we should introduce industrial democracy in our own country. In universities and schools power is similarly passing from staff to students. The solution is to give the students responsibility as well—to introduce democratic procedures for deciding rules of conduct. *The Economist* commended the enterprising and co-operative attitude of students of the Architectural Association School. It made a disparaging comparison with militant students at other educational establishments: 'Just "sitting in" is plainly not AA style.'[1] The moral was missed. AA students already possessed the self-government that militant students elsewhere were trying to secure. If it were true that British citizens and workers were unfit to enjoy direct democracy, the solution would lie in democratizing education. 'We must educate our masters' in the arts of self-government itself.

The state—like a company, a university, a school—is an association of individuals. To establish the referendum as a permanent feature of the Constitution would be important not only for its own sake.

It would symbolize the need and intention to democratize industry and education.

In Britain the state already has a democratic Constitution. But there is evidence, variously in political apathy and militant protest, that it is not democratic enough to satisfy contemporary electors, particularly the younger ones. The two-party system, with its rigorous discipline, has given Government and civil service a power undreamed of by mediaeval Kings. The Establishment and those who identify with it regard the exercise of power by Parliament as presumptuous and by the people as unthinkable. The constant denigration of the referendum by otherwise responsible politicians and writers is as emotional as it is uninformed. Jeremy Thorpe says the whole delicate balance of our Constitution could be upset by the referendum. Let us pray that he is right.

APPENDIX
OTHER COUNTRIES

THE COUNTRIES WHOSE political systems are most comparable to the British are the European democracies, the three Dominions and the United States. This appendix treats of national and federal referenda under their present Constitutions. Lack of constitutional provision does not prevent a country from holding a referendum. Nor does constitutional provision prevent *ad hoc* referenda from being held as well.

AUSTRALIA
Amendments to the Commonwealth (or federal) Constitution must be put to referendum. They are adopted if approved by a majority of those voting and by majorities of those voting in a majority of the States (except that an amendment affecting certain of a State's rights must also be approved by a majority of those voting in that State).

Constitutional amendments are put to referendum if passed by absolute majorities in both Houses. Alternatively, if either House twice, with an interval of three months, passes a constitutional amendment by an absolute majority, the Governor-General may put it to referendum despite rejection by the other House.

There were two Commonwealth referenda before federation, one rejecting and the other accepting a Constitution. During the First World War two *ad hoc* referenda were held on Bills dealing with military service overseas.

BELGIUM
There is no constitutional referendum. A consultative plebiscite was held in 1950 on whether Leopold III should resume his prerogatives. Strong support in Flanders gave him a national majority, but his return was opposed in Wallonia and Brussels. He abdicated later the same year.

CANADA
There is no constitutional provision for federal referenda. Consultative plebiscites were held on Prohibition in 1898 and on overseas service for conscripted men in 1942.

Canadians themselves call such *ad hoc* referenda *plebiscites*, dis-

119

tinguishing them from referenda on legislation provided for in Alberta (and at one time also in British Columbia).

DENMARK

A constitutional amendment must be passed twice by the *Folketing*, the second time within six months of an intervening election, and must also be approved in a referendum by a majority of those voting and 40 per cent of the electorate.

An ordinary Bill (with certain exceptions, notably Money Bills) must be put to referendum at the request of a third of MPs. It will become law unless rejected by a majority of those voting and 30 per cent of the electorate. In an emergency the Royal Assent may be given before the referendum is held, but the Act becomes ineffective if rejected by the requisite simple majority and 30 per cent of the electorate.

If a Bill delegating national sovereignty 'to international authorities set up by mutual agreement with other states for the promotion of international rules of law and co-operation' is passed by five-sixths of all MPs, it can become law without a referendum. If passed by a simple majority of MPs voting (but not by five-sixths of all MPs), such a Bill can then be put to referendum under the provisions for ordinary Bills, not constitutional amendments. Thus national sovereignty may be delegated to an international authority by a simple majority of MPs voting even though it is rejected by a majority of those voting in a referendum with a low turnout.

FINLAND

There is no constitutional provision for the referendum. In a consultative plebiscite in 1931 the electors voted to abolish Prohibition.

FRANCE

A constitutional amendment becomes law if passed by both Assemblies and approved in a referendum. Alternatively the President may submit a constitutional amendment to a joint meeting of both chambers, when it becomes law if it receives three-fifths of the votes cast.

A referendum may also be held on any Bill 'dealing with the organization of the public authorities, approving a Community agreement or authorizing the ratification of a treaty which, although not in conflict with the Constitution, would affect the working of institutions'. This was drafted before the French Community States became independent. The President may put a Bill in any of these categories to referendum on the proposal either of the Government (which virtually means at the President's own wish) or of the two Assemblies. Referenda can only be organized during parliamentary sessions, which gives the Assemblies the opportunity to adopt a motion of censure.

Referenda have been held on the adoption of the Constitution (1958);

Algerian Independence (1961 and 1962); the direct election of the President (1962); regionalization and Senate reform (1969); the extension of the EEC to include Britain, Denmark, Ireland and Norway (1972).

GERMANY (WEST)

Federal legislation changing Land boundaries is subject to referenda in the areas affected. The procedure for the referenda is laid down by federal law. In certain circumstances, if proposed changes are rejected in one or more of the areas affected, they must be reintroduced in the *Bundestag* and, if reinacted, 'shall require approval by referendum throughout the federal territory'. This is the only provision for a federal referendum and none has yet been held.

GREECE

After the fall of the *junta*, the present Greek Parliament was elected under the 1952 Constitution but with the power of a Constituent Assembly to revise it. The Articles relating to the Monarchy were left in abeyance until the plebiscite of December 1974 in which the electors voted for a Republic. This was Greece's sixth plebiscite on the Monarchy. The Constitution does not include the constitutional referendum; nor is there any intention to introduce it.

HOLLAND

The Constitution has no provision for the referendum. Nor has a referendum been held under it.

IRELAND

A constitutional amendment must be endorsed in a referendum by a simple majority of those voting.

A majority of the members of the Senate and not less than a third of the members of the *Dáil* may jointly petition the President to decline to sign and promulgate any Bill on the ground that it 'contains a proposal of such national importance that the will of the people thereon ought to be ascertained'. If the President is persuaded, he must not sign the Bill until it has been approved by the electorate in a referendum or reaffirmed in the *Dáil* after a general election. This provision of the constitution has not yet been invoked.

ITALY

Constitutional amendments and other defined constitutional Bills must be passed by both chambers of the legislature in two successive sessions at an interval of not less than three months and be approved by an absolute majority of the members of each chamber after a second reading. If approved by two-thirds of the members of each chamber, they must become law. If approved by absolute majorities but not by two-thirds of the members of each chamber, they must be put to referendum on a demand of a fifth of the members of either chamber, or of 500,000 electors, or of five Regional Councils. A Bill submitted to referendum becomes law if approved by a majority of those voting.

An ordinary Bill or measure which will have the force of law (other than a fiscal or budgetary measure, an amnesty, pardon, or Bill ratifying an international treaty) must be put to referendum on the demand of 500,000 electors or of five Regional Councils (but not outside a parliamentary session or during the first year of Parliament's life). It becomes law if it is approved by a majority of those voting and if a majority of the electors vote.

The only referendum held under the present Constitution was that on divorce in 1974. A plebiscite in 1946 (when there was a Constituent Assembly) established a Republic in place of the Monarchy.

Italy also has the initiative: 50,000 electors may introduce a Bill drafted in the form of articles.

LUXEMBOURG

An amendment to the Constitution in May 1919 provided that 'The electorate may be called upon to make known its views by way of referendum in cases and under conditions to be determined by the law.' In two referenda held on 28 September 1919 the electors voted for the maintenance of the Monarchy with Princess Charlotte as Grand Duchess and for a customs union with France and not Belgium. In a third referendum in June 1937 a Bill already passed by Parliament, providing for coercive measures against revolutionary parties in general and the Communist Party in particular, was rejected by about 51 per cent of those voting.

Because no general law about referenda has been passed since the original constitutional amendment in May 1919, the Luxembourg referendum must be categorized as consultative. In every case the Government respected the wishes of the electorate (except that it proved impossible to negotiate a customs union with France and one was therefore negotiated with Belgium instead). Whereas the referenda on the Monarchy and the customs union were understood to be consultative, that on coercive measures against revolutionary parties (rejected by the narrowest of margins) seems to have been treated as binding.

NEW ZEALAND

A Licensing Act in 1911 provided for referenda on liquor control. Though a number were held, the 60 per cent of votes required for Prohibition was never achieved. The Electoral Act 1956 provided that certain of its own sections could be repealed or amended only with the support of three-quarters of MPs voting or by referendum.

Ad hoc referenda have also been held, for example under the Gaming Poll Act 1948 and the Military Training Poll Act 1949. Acts providing for *ad hoc* referenda usually adopt the procedural provisions applicable to the licensing referenda.

NORWAY

Norway's referendum on the EEC in 1972 was its fifth plebiscite. Others were held on union with Sweden (August 1905), the election of Prince Carl of Denmark as King of Norway (November 1905), the Prohibition of spirits and strong wines (1919 and 1926). The first two were binding and the others consultative. There is no constitutional referendum.

PORTUGAL

Elections were held in April 1975 for a Constituent Assembly which will draw up a new Constitution. The previous Constitution was approved in 1933 in a plebiscite of problematical legitimacy.

SWEDEN

According to the 1975 Constitution, 'Provisions for an advisory referendum throughout the country shall be laid down in law.' Since in fact there is no standing legislation, this is merely symbolic, like the 1922 constitutional amendment allowing the King and the *Riksdag* (Parliament) to order a referendum. Swedish referenda are consultative only, and there are no circumstances in which it is obligatory to hold one. Three have been held: on Prohibition (1922); on driving on the right instead of the left (1955); on three different national pensions schemes (1957). The original assumption was that the *Riksdag* would honour a clear majority in a referendum. Although, however, an overwhelming majority voted to continue driving on the left in 1955, the Government and three Opposition parties agreed together in 1967 that they should be made to drive on the right.

SWITZERLAND

A Federal law or decree or an international treaty concluded for an unspecified period or for more than fifteen years must be put to referendum if 30,000 electors or eight cantons demand it. Its acceptance or rejection is determined by a simple majority of the electors voting.

Any constitutional amendment must be put to referendum. It will be adopted only if approved by a majority of those voting and by majorities of those voting in a majority of the cantons.

An emergency decree may be brought into force even though 30,000 electors or eight cantons demand that it be put to referendum. A referendum must be held, however, and, if the decree is rejected, it cannot continue in operation for more than a year.

If an emergency decree conflicts with the Constitution, it must be treated as an amendment and put to referendum even if no elector objects to it. Unless it is approved by a majority of those voting and by majorities in a majority of the cantons, it cannot continue in operation for more than a year.

Constitutional amendments may be initiated by 50,000 electors. There are provisions for dealing with both general proposals and complete drafts.

There is no provision for initiatives of non-constitutional legislation. Nor, however, is there any restriction on what may be added to the Constitution. Hence 50,000 electors may initiate any legislation by calling it a constitutional amendment (which is how the Constitution comes to contain a clause on the slaughtering of animals). Since the result of the ensuing referendum is binding, it follows that the Swiss electorate may at any time pass legislation even though it be rejected by both chambers of the Federal Assembly.

TURKEY

The Constitution of the Republic of Turkey was endorsed in a plebiscite in 1961. There is no provision in the Constitution for any further referenda.

UNITED STATES

There is no constitutional provision for a federal referendum. Nor has one ever been held. This is despite prolific experience of the referendum and initiative in member States.

NOTES

1 THE REFERENDUM IN PERSPECTIVE

1 A. V. Dicey, a symposium on 'The Referendum', *National Review*, March 1894
2 *The Guardian*, 28 November 1974
3 Report of the *Royal Commission on the Constitution 1969-1973 Volume II Memorandum of Dissent*, HMSO, London, Cmnd. 5460-1, October 1973, p. 34
4 *Ibid.*, p. 34
5 *Ibid.*, pp. 34-5
6 *Ibid.*, p. 60
7 Quoted *ibid.*, p. 33
8 Quoted in Uwe Kitzinger, *Diplomacy and Persuasion: How Britain Joined the Common Market*, Thames and Hudson, London 1973, p. 419
9 Quoted *ibid.*, p. 420
10 Speech 'To the Electors of Bristol, on his being declared by the sheriffs, duly elected one of the representatives in Parliament for that city, on Thursday the third of November, 1774', *Works*, vol. I, Bohn's Standard Library, George Bell and Sons, London 1902, p. 447
11 Jean Jacques Rousseau, *The Social Contract and Discourses*, translated with introduction by G. D. H. Cole, Dent, London 1913, p. 78
12 *Op. cit.*, p. 447
13 18 October 1974
14 12 October 1974

2 ORIGINS

1 George Willis Botsford, *The Roman Assemblies: From Their Origin to the End of the Republic*, Macmillan Co. New York 1909, p. 211
2 *Ibid.*, p. 178
3 See W. A. B. Coolidge, 'The Early History of the Referendum', *English Historical Review*, October 1891
4 Oscar and Mary Handlin, *The Popular Sources of Political Authority: Documents on the Massachusetts Constitution of 1780*, Belknap Press of Harvard University Press, Cambridge, Massachusetts, 1966, p. 172
5 Quoted in Léon Duguit and Henry Monnier, *Les Constitutions et Les*

Principales Lois Politiques de la France depuis 1789, Librairie Générale de Droit et de Jurisprudence, Paris, fourth edition 1925, p. 36

6 Quoted in A. Esmein, *Éléments de Droit Constitutionnel Français et Comparé*, Librairie de la Société du Recueil Général des Lois et des Arrêts, Paris 1895, third edition 1903, p. 261

7 Duguit and Monnier, *op. cit.*, p. xxxiii

8 Article 19, quoted *ibid.*, p. 79

9 Letter of 5 April 1798 from the Swiss to the French Directory, quoted in Simon Deploige, *The Referendum in Switzerland*, translated by C. P. Trevelyan, Longmans, London 1898, p. 19

10 Quoted *ibid.*, p. 83

3 LOCAL REFERENDA

1 Josef Redlich and Francis W. Hirst, *The History of Local Government in England*, with an introduction and epilogue by Bryan Keith-Lucas, Macmillan, London 1958, second edition 1970, p. 31

2 Sidney and Beatrice Webb, *The History of Liquor Licensing Principally from 1700 to 1830*, Longmans, London 1903, p. 62

3 See *Report of the Departmental Committee on Scottish Licensing Law*, HMSO, London, Cmnd. 5354, August 1973, pp. 158-64

4 See E. P. Hennock, *Fit and Proper Persons: Ideal and Reality in Nineteenth-Century Urban Government*, Edward Arnold, London 1973, p. 298

5 Thomas Kelly, *A History of Public Libraries in Great Britain 1845-1965*, The Library Association, London 1973, p. 111

6 HMSO, London, Third Schedule, Part vi, Section 5(4)

7 *Hansard*, House of Commons, 27 May 1932, HMSO, London, 5th ser., vol. 266, cols. 721-2

8 *Hansard*, House of Commons, 29 June 1932, HMSO, London, 5th ser., vol. 267, col. 1950

9 *Halifax Courier and Guardian* (now the *Evening Courier*), 16 January 1947

10 *Ibid.*

11 *Halifax Courier and Guardian*, 8 February 1947

12 12 July 1965

13 30 June 1970

14 This point was made by Sir Basil Peto, Conservative MP for Barnstaple, during the second-reading debate on the Sunday Entertainments Bill 1932. See *Hansard*, House of Commons, 27 May, HMSO, London, 5th ser., vol. 266, col. 728

4 IRELAND

1 See A. V. Dicey, 'Ought the Referendum To Be Introduced in England?', *Contemporary Review*, April 1890

2 F. W. Hirst, 'Mr. Gladstone's Fourth Premiership and Final Retire-

ment, 1892-1897', in Sir Wemyss Reid (ed.), *The Life of William Ewart Gladstone*, Cassell, London 1899, p. 722

3 A. V. Dicey, a symposium on 'The Referendum', *National Review*, March 1894

4 R. C. K. Ensor, *England 1870-1914*, Oxford University Press, Oxford 1936, p. 476

5 *Hansard*, House of Commons, 24 March 1972, HMSO, London, 5th ser., vol. 833, col. 1862

6 *Hansard*, House of Commons, 3 July 1973, HMSO, London, 5th ser., vol. 859, col. 311

5 NATIONAL REFERENDA THAT MIGHT HAVE BEEN

1 'The Agreement of the People as presented to the Council of the Army', Samuel Rawson Gardiner (ed.), *The Constitutional Documents of the Puritan Revolution 1625-1660*, The Clarendon Press, Oxford 1889, third edition 1906, p. 334

2 'The Agreement of the People', *ibid.*, p. 366

3 Richard Shannon, *The Crisis of Imperialism 1865-1915*, Hart-Davis, MacGibbon, London 1974, p. 245

4 Roy Jenkins, *Mr. Balfour's Poodle: An Account of the Struggle between the House of Lords and the Government of Mr. Asquith*, Heinemann, London 1954, p. 105

5 See Robert Blake, *The Unknown Prime Minister: The Life and Times of Andrew Bonar Law 1858-1923*, Eyre and Spottiswoode, London 1955, pp. 111-12

6 Quoted in Philip Goodhart, *Referendum*, Tom Stacey, London 1971, pp. 43-4

7 Quoted in Robert James (ed.), *Memoirs of a Conservative: J. C. C. Davidson's Memoirs and Papers, 1910-37*, Weidenfeld and Nicolson, London 1969, p. 332

8 Quoted in Keith Middlemas and John Barnes, *Baldwin: A Biography*, Weidenfeld and Nicolson, London 1969, p. 571

9 Quoted *ibid.*, p. 576

10 C. R. Attlee, *As It Happened*, Heinemann, London 1954, p. 137

11 Sidney and Beatrice Webb, Longmans, London. See second edition 1902, pp. 19-27, 30-7, 60-4

12 Clifford D. Sharp, Fabian Tract No. 155, The Fabian Society, London, p. 6

6 MARKET MEMBERSHIP

1 *Hansard*, House of Commons, 17 July 1967, HMSO, London, 5th ser., vol. 750, col. 1450

2 *Ibid.*, col. 1454

3 *Hansard*, House of Commons, 25 November 1969, HMSO, London, 5th ser., vol. 792, col. 199

4 *Ibid.*, col. 200

5   *Hansard*, House of Commons, 10 December 1969, HMSO, London, 5th ser., vol. 793, col. 442
6   *Ibid.*, col. 442
7   *Op. cit.*
8   *Hansard*, House of Commons, 24 February 1970, HMSO, London, 5th ser., vol. 796, col. 1019
9   Quoted in Goodhart, *op. cit.*, p. 60
10 *The Common Market: Questions and answers*, pp. 50-51
11 *Ibid.*, p. 51
12 *The Guardian*, 9 June 1973
13 *The Guardian*, 24 February 1974
14 *Ibid.*
15 *The Guardian*, 17 July 1974
16 Quoted in *Socialist Commentary*, October 1974
17 *The Guardian*, 29 September 1974
18 *The Guardian*, 23 September 1974
19 *The Guardian*, 26 September 1974
20 *Ibid.*
21 *The Guardian*, 27 September 1974
22 *The Guardian*, 2 October 1974
23 In an interview on Thames Television, 21 November 1974, quoted in *The Guardian*, 22 November 1974
24 *The Guardian*, 26 October 1974
25 *Murder in the Cathedral*, Part I, *The Collected Poems and Plays of T. S. Eliot*, Faber, London 1969, p. 258

7   ALIEN TO REPRESENTATIVE GOVERNMENT?

1   Burke, *op. cit.*, vol. 1, p. 447
2   Speech 'At His Arrival at Bristol', *ibid.*, p. 440
3   See A. V. Dicey, 'The Referendum and Its Critics', *The Quarterly Review*, April 1910
4   H. McD. Clokie, *Canadian Government and Politics*, Longmans, Toronto 1944, p. 85
5   See *op. cit.*, p. 17
6   See *The Sunday Times*, 26 January 1975
7   *Free and Swiss: The Story of Switzerland*, adapted and translated from the German by R. P. Heller and E. Long, Oswald Wolff, London 1970, p. 125
8   A. V. Dicey, a symposium on 'The Referendum', *National Review*, 1894
9   Quoted by Peter Niesewand, *The Guardian*, 27 November 1974
10 *The Sunday Times*, 10 November 1974

8   ALIEN TO THE BRITISH CONSTITUTION?

1   *The Guardian*, 8 November 1974
2   'Any Questions?', Radio 4, 27 September 1974

3 *The Guardian*, 4 December 1974
4 See A. V. Dicey, *Introduction to the Study of the Law of the Constitution*, edited by E. C. S. Wade, Macmillan, London 1885, ninth edition 1939, pp. 64-70. Dicey attributed the dictum to Alpheus Todd, who in his *Parliamentary Government in the British Colonies* (Little, Brown, Boston 1880, p. 192) wrote: 'It is equally certain that a Parliament cannot so bind its successors by the terms of any statute, as to limit the discretion of a future Parliament ...' In addition to quoting judicial precedents, Todd invoked Edmund Burke's comments on the Act of Union. But Burke said Parliament *would* not bind its successors rather than could not: 'What shall we think of the wisdom (to say nothing of the competence) of that Legislature, which should ordain to itself such a fundamental Law at its outset, as to disable itself from executing its own functions; which should prevent it from making any further Laws, however wanted ...' (speech 'On the Acts of Uniformity', 1772, *Works*, vol. x, c. and j. Rivington, London 1826, p. 7)
5 See *Hansard*, House of Commons, 28 October 1971, HMSO, London, 5th ser., vol. 823, col. 2103
6 5 August 1974
7 *Op. cit.*, p. 68n
8 See W. Ivor Jennings, *The Law and the Constitution*, University of London Press, London 1933, second edition 1938, p. 149
9 *Hansard*, House of Commons, 3 July 1973, HMSO, London, 5th ser., vol. 859, col. 280
10 *Ibid.*, col. 283
11 29 September 1974

9 IMPROPER INFLUENCES

1 *An Authentic Copy of the New Plan of the French Constitution, as presented to the National Convention, by the Committee of Constitution, to which is prefixed The Speech of M. Condorcet, on Friday, February 15, 1793 (M. BREARD, President,) delivered in the name of the Committee of Constitution*, London 1973, p. vii. Condorcet was presenting the (subsequently rejected) Girondin Constitution
2 Chapman and Hall, London 1918, p. 37
3 George Martin, *The Red Shirt and the Cross of Savoy: The Story of Italy's Risorgimento (1748-1871)*, Eyre and Spottiswoode, London 1970, p. 615
4 HMSO, London, Cmnd. 5925, February 1975, p. 4
5 See Strachey, *op. cit.*, p. 73
6 See Public Libraries Act 1892, First Schedule
7 Postal ballot-paper for referenda held on 18 May 1974
8 *Op. cit.*, p. 7

10 ALTERNATIVES TO THE REFERENDUM

1 *The Economist*, 30 June 1974
2 See *The Guardian*, 17 July 1974
3 'Do We Need a Referendum?', *Contemporary Review*, September 1972
4 *How Democracies Vote: A Study of Majority and Proportional Electoral Systems*, Faber, London 1955 (with James Lambert under the title *Voting in Democracies*), third edition 1970, p. 125
5 See 'Do We Need a Referendum?', *Contemporary Review*, September 1972

11 SUITABLE SUBJECTS

1 'Joining the Six—the case for a referendum', 1 August 1970
2 *The Guardian*, 17 July 1974
3 Thürer, *op. cit.*, p. 124
4 *Hansard*, House of Commons, 17 July 1967, HMSO, London, 5th ser., vol. 750, cols. 1450-1
5 HMSO, London, Section 2(1)
6 Simon Winchester, *The Guardian*, 14 January 1975
7 'On Liberty', *Selected Writings of John Stuart Mill*, edited by Maurice Cowling, Mentor, London 1968, p. 132

12 WHO DECIDES ON A REFERENDUM?

1 *Hansard*, House of Lords, 5 July 1973, HMSO, London, 5th ser., vol. 344, col. 404
2 Constitution of Ireland, Article 27(1)
3 *Op. cit.*, p. 137
4 Crowther-Hunt and Peacock, *op. cit.*, p. 8
5 *Direct Legislation by the People*, versus *Representative Government*, translated from the original Swiss pamphlets by Eugene Oswald, London 1869, p. 14
6 'Power to the People, not to MPs', *Liberal News*, 18 February 1975
7 *Ibid.*
8 Quoted in E. Ramón Arango, *Leopold III and the Belgian Royal Question*, John Hopkins, Baltimore 1961, p. 188

13 WHAT WILL REFERENDA ACHIEVE?

1 13 March 1971

SUGGESTIONS FOR FURTHER READING

SWITZERLAND

Simon Deploige, *The Referendum in Switzerland*, translated by C. P. Trevelyan, edited with notes, introduction and appendices by Lilian Tomn, Longmans, London 1898

Christopher Hughes, *The Federal Constitution of Switzerland*, The Clarendon Press, Oxford 1954

UNITED STATES

V. O. Key, Jr. and Winston W. Crouch, *The Initiative and the Referendum in California*, University of California Press and Cambridge University Press, Berkeley and London 1939

Ellis Paxson Oberholtzer, *The Referendum in America together with some Chapters on the Initiative and the Recall*, Charles Scribner's Sons, New York 1910, second edition 1912

UNITED KINGDOM

Referendum

Philip Goodhart, *Referendum*, Tom Stacey, London 1971

John St Loe Strachey, *The Referendum: A Handbook to the Poll of the People, Referendum, or Democratic Right of Veto on Leglisation*, T. Fisher Unwin, London 1924

Participation

Lord Crowther-Hunt and Professor A. T. Peacock, Report of the *Royal Commission on the Constitution 1969-1973 Volume II Memorandum of Dissent*, HMSO, London, Cmnd. 5460-1, 1973

Cecil S. Emden. *The People and the Constitution: Being a History of the Development of the People's Influence in British Government*, The Clarendon Press, Oxford 1933, second edition 1956

PLEBISCITES

Philip Goodhart, *Referendum*, Tom Stacey, London 1971

Sarah Wambaugh, *A Monograph on Plebiscites With a Collection of Official Documents*, Oxford University Press, New York 1920

SINGLE TRANSFERABLE VOTE

Enid Lakeman, *How Democracies Vote: A Study of Majority and Proportional Systems*, Faber, London 1955 (with James Lambert under the title *Voting in Democracies*), third edition 1970

INDEX